WELCOME

Livewires

Get into the Bible

This book is an adventure story, an activity book and a fact-finding book about the Bible all in one. The contents page will help you find out about a particular part of the Bible, or you can follow the Livewires' adventure right through by reading Get into the Bible as a storybook.

Whatever you choose to do, don't forget to stop on the factfile pages where you'll find lots of puzzles to help you remember what a fantastic book the Bible is.

There is also a Bible library to make as you go along. To do this, you'll need to start collecting empty matchboxes, or boxes of a similar size. You will need sixty-six altogether! You can make each book as you go along by covering the box with plain paper and writing the name on the spine. Use cereal boxes of equal sizes to make the bookshelves to keep your Bible books on. Cut off one face of each box and make strips from this piece to make the shelves. Just add another bookshelf once you have filled each one with books. When you have finished all sixty-six you could put them in sections, just like a real library—you'll learn how to do this as you follow the Livewires' adventure.

If you've got a Bible you could look up the references on Boot's screen. Boot will show you how...

Boot's right! And you can find any verse in the Bible the same way!

FACTFILE

PSALM 119:89

The contents page in your Bible will tell you where to find the book of Psalms. The next number tells you which Psalm it is (119 in this case) and the number after the colon (:) tells you which verse of that Psalm you need to read.

Text copyright © Sheryl Herbert 1998
Illustrations copyright © Simon Smith 1998

The author asserts the moral right to
be identified as the author of this work

Published by
The Bible Reading Fellowship
Peter's Way, Sandy Lane West
Oxford OX4 5HG
ISBN 0 7459 3563 X

First edition 1998

10 9 8 7 6 5 4 3 2 1 0

Acknowledgments

Unless otherwise stated, scripture quotations are taken from the Good News Bible published by The Bible Societies/ HarperCollins Publishers Ltd UK © American Bible Society, 1966, 1971, 1976, 1992.

A catalogue record for this book
is available from the British Library

Printed and bound in Malta
by Interprint Limited

CONTENTS

The Livewires were enjoying a peaceful afternoon in the park when Quartz suddenly cried out that she had to go home and sort out a costume! The Livewires looked at her in amazement.
It's Book Week at school and we've got to dress up as a character from a book. I don't know who to go as.
Yeah, our class is having a quiz. We've all got to take a question about a book—if no one can answer your question, you win a prize. I'm trying to think of a really hard one.

As Quartz and Tim were talking about Book Week, the others joined in. It was Book Week for all of them. They decided to go to Annie-log's and use Boot, the computer, to help them.

Before Annie-log had finished typing instructions, Boot started scrolling through his fact file.
World's Number One Best Seller
A Library
66 Books in One
Mentioned in
Guinness Book of Records

The Livewires sat watching until the last message appeared.
PSALM 119:89
Your word, O Lord, will last forever; it is eternal in heaven.
The Bible!
I never thought of that book!

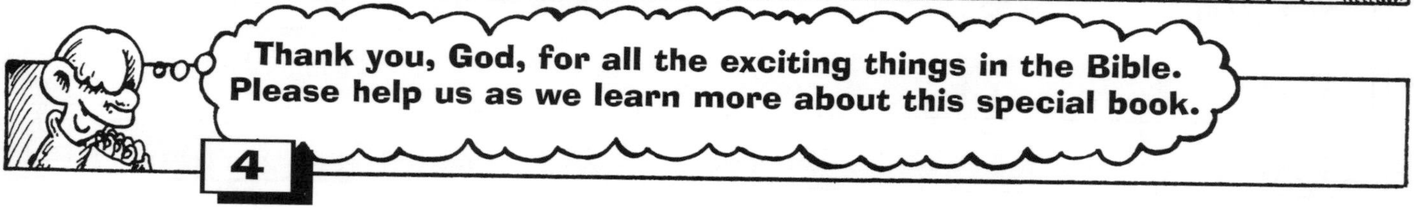
Thank you, God, for all the exciting things in the Bible. Please help us as we learn more about this special book.

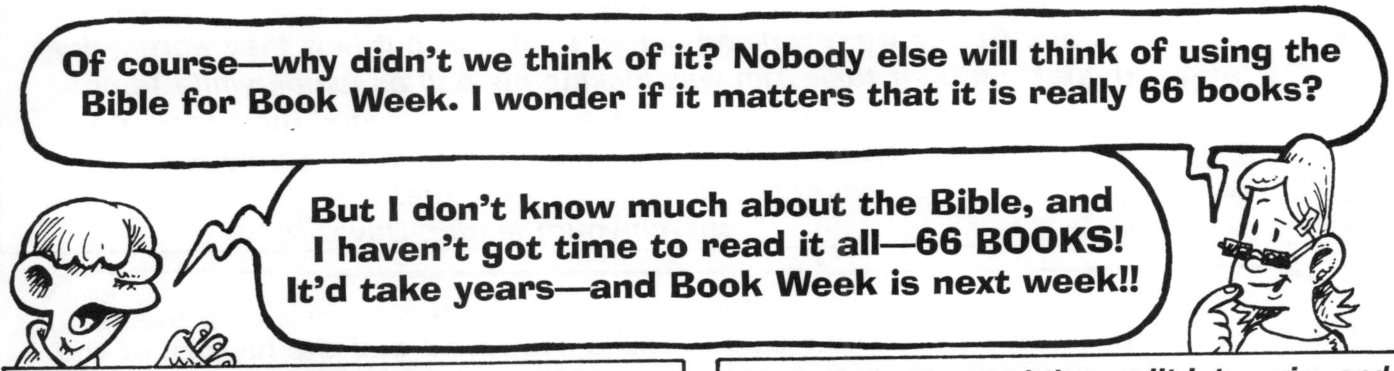
Of course—why didn't we think of it? Nobody else will think of using the Bible for Book Week. I wonder if it matters that it is really 66 books?
But I don't know much about the Bible, and I haven't got time to read it all—66 BOOKS! It'd take years—and Book Week is next week!!

Annie-log typed in 'BIBLE' to see what Boot would come up with.
OLD TESTAMENT
NEW TESTAMENT
Wonder what the Old and New Testaments are?

Annie-log suggested they split into pairs and find out about the Bible.
PSALM 119:105
Your word is a lamp to guide me and a light for my path.

As the Livewires looked at Boot's screen they began to realize that the Bible was more than just an ordinary book. They were excited about what they were going to discover.

While the Livewires start their work, can you think of all the different forms of light we have? You may like to draw some of them after you have found them hidden in this wordsearch.

C	D	M	G	F	L	M	N	O	P
H	E	A	D	L	I	G	H	T	S
L	V	T	U	O	T	S	R	Q	U
A	W	C	X	O	Y	M	O	O	N
S	E	H	D	D	C	B	A	Z	C
E	O	I	L	L	A	M	P	F	A
R	J	I	F	I	R	E	H	G	N
B	K	L	M	G	N	O	P	S	D
E	W	V	U	H	T	S	R	Q	L
A	X	Y	Z	T	O	R	C	H	E
M	A	B	C	S	D	E	F	G	S

The hidden words are: torch, match, fire, candles, sun, moon, headlights, oil lamp, floodlights, laser beam.

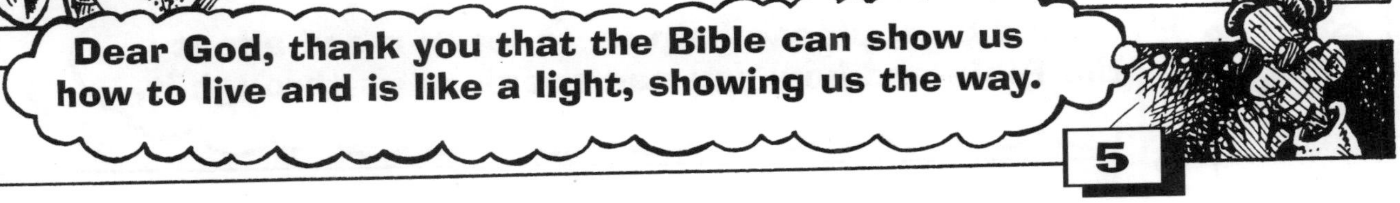
Dear God, thank you that the Bible can show us how to live and is like a light, showing us the way.

Tim and Quartz were walking home, talking about how they were going to start on their task. Tim was kicking his ball as usual, while Tempo trotted beside him, quietly for a change. They decided they needed to talk to someone who knew more about the Bible than they did. They eventually decided to go to their church youth leader, Dave.
The Old Testament has 39 books in it and starts with the book of Genesis. It begins with stories about how God created the world and the history of the people of Israel, God's chosen people. Some stories are happy and some are sad. Jesus called the Old Testament 'the Scriptures'. It was the only part of the Bible written at that time.
Dave explained that the word 'Testament' means an agreement.
You mean, like me agreeing to be in the football team?
Yes, that's right. You've agreed to play on Saturday—so you make sure you're there.
That's like a promise.
Yes, the story of the Old Testament is the story of God's promise to be with his chosen people, Israel.
Dave opened his Bible and Quartz read the words:
Exodus 19:5
The whole creation is mine, but you will be my chosen people.
HOLY BIBLE
Lord God, please help us to learn more about the Bible and how you can speak to us through it.

Dave explained that the Old Testament is important because it traces the history of the Jewish people right back over more than a thousand years and helps us to understand how God was at work in the lives of people before Jesus was born.

As I said, the Old Testament contains 39 books and they're all different. They aren't all written by the same person. The Bible is often called 'God's Word', because Christians believe that when people wrote the Bible, they were helped by God to write the truth.

Dave then read them another verse:

2 Timothy 3:16
All Scripture is inspired by God and is useful for teaching the truth, rebuking error, correcting faults, and giving instruction for right living.

Tim and Quartz suddenly remembered they were supposed to be detectives, so they quickly started to write all they had found out, so that they could report back to the others.

Tim and Quartz have found out so many things, they're a bit confused. Can you help them sort out a few things before they report back to the others? Look back over the last couple of pages and decide if what Tim and Quartz have written is True or False. You are now the detectives!

1. There are 99 books in the Bible.

2. The Bible has an Old Testament and a New Testament.

3. The first book of the Bible is called Genesis.

4. The Old Testament tells stories about the life of Jesus.

5. The Bible is the Number 2 Best Seller.

6. There are 66 books in the Old Testament.

7. The people of Israel are God's chosen people.

8. All the stories in the Bible are written by one person.

9. God helped people write the Bible.

10. The Bible is often called 'God's Word'.

How did you get on? You should have 5 True and 5 False.

Annie-log and Little Ben were using Boot to help them with their task. They had to find out about the books of the Law. The books of the Law had a special name—the Pentateuch—and were the first five books of the Bible. They had even learnt the names off by heart to impress the others—Genesis, Exodus, Leviticus, Numbers and Deuteronomy (they had a bit of trouble saying that one!) These books contain the stories of God's people from Abraham to Moses. Annie-log wanted to find out more about these people and started to type 'ABRA...'
There was a bleep and a buzz from Boot, and names started scrolling down the screen!
These don't look like any names I know! Oh, Boot, don't go all wrong now!
AHAMABR, RAHSA, AACIS, COBJA, AUES, EPHJOS.
While Annie-log and Little Ben sat staring at the screen wondering what to do, there was another bleep from Boot! When they looked they saw Boot had given them a clue.
First half last, second half first.
POP
What on earth does that mean?
Can you work out the clue?

I've got it! Look at the second half of the word and put it at the front. Then we've got the proper names.

Boot then gave another bleep. A verse appeared on his screen.

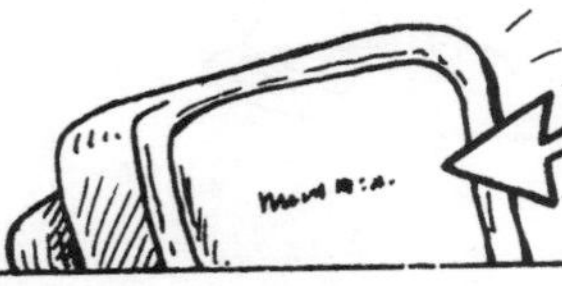

GENESIS 15:5

Annie-log read it out:

The Lord said to Abraham, 'Look at the sky and try to count the stars; you will have as many descendants as that.'

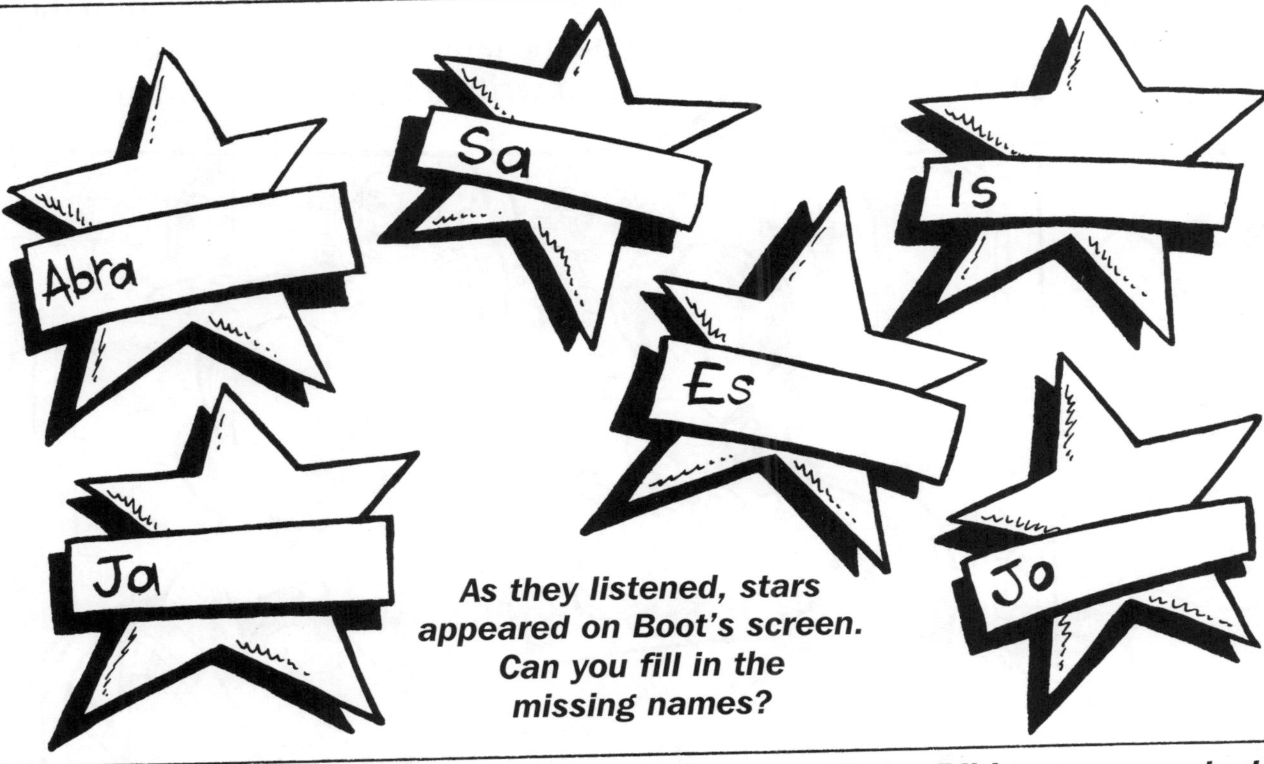

As they listened, stars appeared on Boot's screen. Can you fill in the missing names?

Now that you know the names of the first five books of the Bible, you can start making your library. Make five boxes from the diagram at the beginning of the book and write the name of each of the Pentateuch books on the spine.

See how many words you can make out of the word

P E N T A T E U C H

Thank you, God, that we can learn about people who followed you so long ago.

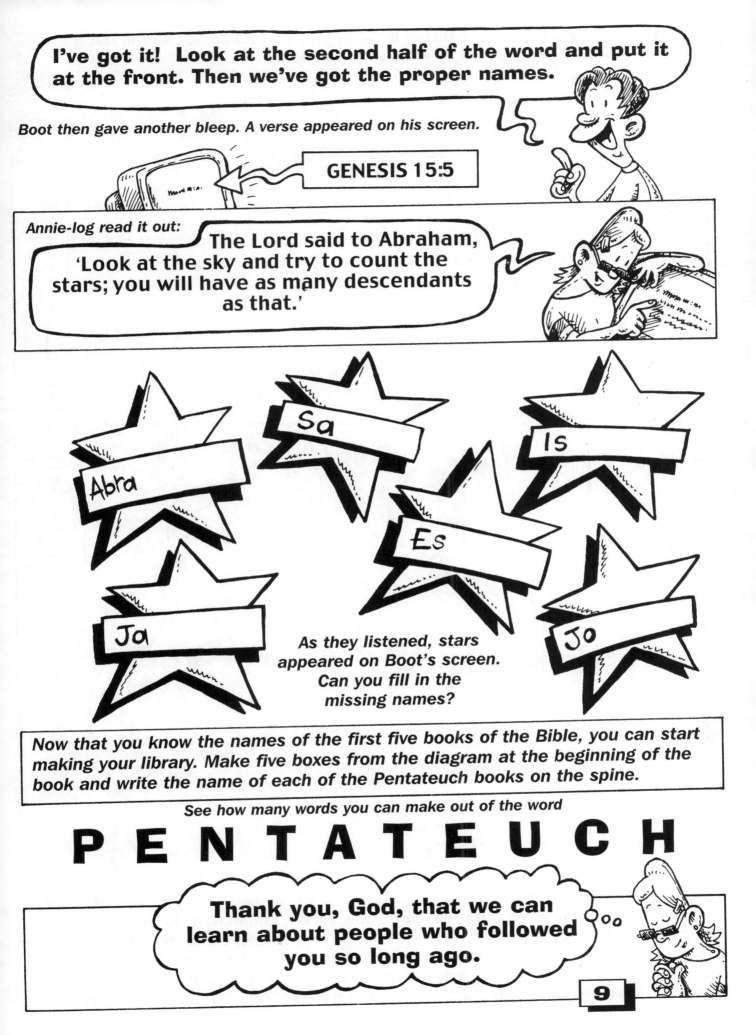

Annie-log and Little Ben were amazed by what they had found out so far, but they had a few questions to ask, so they too went to see Dave.

Dave told Annie-log and Little Ben that Joseph had become Prime Minister of Egypt and saved his family when there was a famine. All his family went to live in Egypt. After Joseph's family had died, there was a new king in Egypt who did not like the Israelites living there. God chose Moses to take the Israelites out of Egypt. The stories of their travels in the desert are in the book of Exodus. While they were still travelling through the desert, God gave them ten rules to show them how he wanted them to live.

The laws that God gave to Moses are what we call the Ten Commandments. They are the rules God wants us to follow. They tell us that we should only worship God, and how we should care for each other.

Little Ben decided to write some of his own rules.
He wrote:
1. Be kind to animals.
2. Don't throw litter.

Can you think of any rules you would have in order to help others enjoy life? Write them down on these stepping stones.

Dear Lord God, help me to know how you want me to care for others.

Data and Digit hadn't been very pleased when Annie-log asked them to find out about the history books, particularly when they found out there were twelve of them—Joshua, Judges, Ruth, 1 Samuel, 2 Samuel, 1 Kings, 2 Kings, 1 Chronicles, 2 Chronicles, Ezra, Nehemiah and Esther. They decided to learn the names of six books each! However, they soon discovered that the history books were full of exciting stories and so they each decided to dress up as one of the people from these books.

Digit was dressed as an Israelite man. He carried a trumpet as a clue for everyone to guess who he was.

The children tried to guess who Digit was, but no one had any real idea.

I'm Joshua.
Joshua 6:20: So the priests blew the trumpets. As soon as the men heard it, they gave a loud shout, and the walls collapsed. Then all the army went straight up the hill into the city and captured it.

Most of the children hadn't heard of Joshua, so Digit told them all he knew about this man.

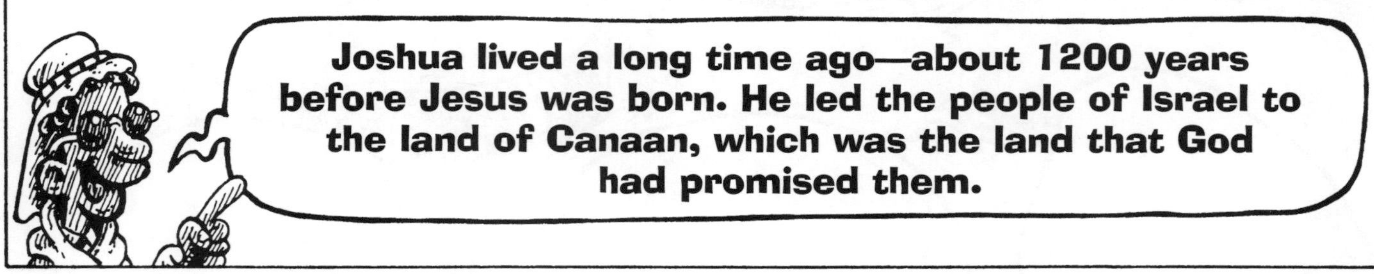
Joshua lived a long time ago—about 1200 years before Jesus was born. He led the people of Israel to the land of Canaan, which was the land that God had promised them.

Joshua had captured the city of Jericho. He and his soldiers marched around the city every day for six days. On the seventh day they marched around the city seven times while the priests blew their trumpets. After the seventh time on the seventh day, Joshua gave a shout and the walls fell down—so Joshua and his soldiers were able to capture the city.

Perhaps you would like to colour in the picture of Digit dressed as Joshua.

Data had a thought: Joshua trusted God when he walked around the walls of Jericho, even though he didn't know what was going to happen. In what ways do you think you might do the same?

The fancy dress parade was very good. Children were dressed in all sorts of clothes.

There were Little Red Riding Hood, The Twits, Mr. Majeika, Just William and lots more. The children were having a wonderful time guessing who everyone was and hearing a little bit about each story or character. Soon it was Data's turn. She walked on to the stage wearing an old tunic and carrying a small toy lamb and a catapult. There were a lot of guesses, but no one knew who she was, so she gave them this clue:

1 Samuel 17:40: He took his shepherd's stick and then picked up five smooth stones from the stream and put them in his bag. With his catapult ready, he went to meet Goliath.
BOOK WEEK

As soon as she said 'Goliath', lots of hands went up. They knew she was David, the shepherd boy who killed the Philistine giant, Goliath. Data was asked to tell them about her character.

David was brought up to be a shepherd boy, but was chosen to be the King of Israel. He was a brave soldier and a great king. He liked music and wrote many prayers and psalms. David trusted in God, and knew that God would be with him and help him, even in hard times.

Soon it was time to go home. Everyone had enjoyed the day and had learnt something new. Data and Digit were looking forward to telling the rest of the Livewires what they had found out.

Colour in the picture of Data.

Help me, Father God, to trust you like David did. Amen

Tim and Quartz were already finding out about the next five books in the Bible—Job, Psalms, Proverbs, Ecclesiastes and The Song of Songs. These books are called the books of Poetry and Wisdom.

Tim decided he was going to find a question from these books to ask at school. He thought no one would be able to answer—not even his teacher. He and Quartz started on their research.

They looked first at the book of Job and discovered it was the story of a good man who had everything taken away from him. His friends weren't very helpful and said that he must have done something bad. Job continued to trust God, even though it wasn't easy and he was very angry about what had happened.

Quartz thought she had found a question for Tim. 'What is a psalm?' she said. Tim wasn't too sure, so they looked in the book of Psalms. There were 150. Some were very long but others were quite short. They both found a psalm they knew.

Psalm 23:1
The Lord is my shepherd: I have everything I need.

As Tim and Quartz read the psalm right through, they remembered their leader at church telling them that this psalm was written by the shepherd boy who became king.

That's who Data dressed up as!
I like this psalm because it helps me remember that God is with me all the time, and he will never leave me.
Yeah, me too. But that question's not hard enough. I think I've got one, though.
BIBLE

Tim wouldn't tell Quartz what his question was. Can you guess from the clue he gave her? He has muddled up the letters of the book—

SPREBROV

How are you getting on with your Bible library? You should have made 17 boxes altogether, and written the names on them. Now you can make the next five and label them.

There was great excitement as the quiz began. The first few questions were easy: Who wrote 'James and the Giant Peach'? Which bear likes honey? Who put a mouse in a sweet jar?

Tim was sure he would beat everyone. He walked to the front and read his question out.
Who wrote these words, found in a very famous book: 'No one who gossips can be trusted with a secret'?

Everyone was quiet as they thought about the question. Slowly a few hands went up and some answers were given—Queen Elizabeth, Winston Churchill, Enid Blyton and Dick King-Smith were some.

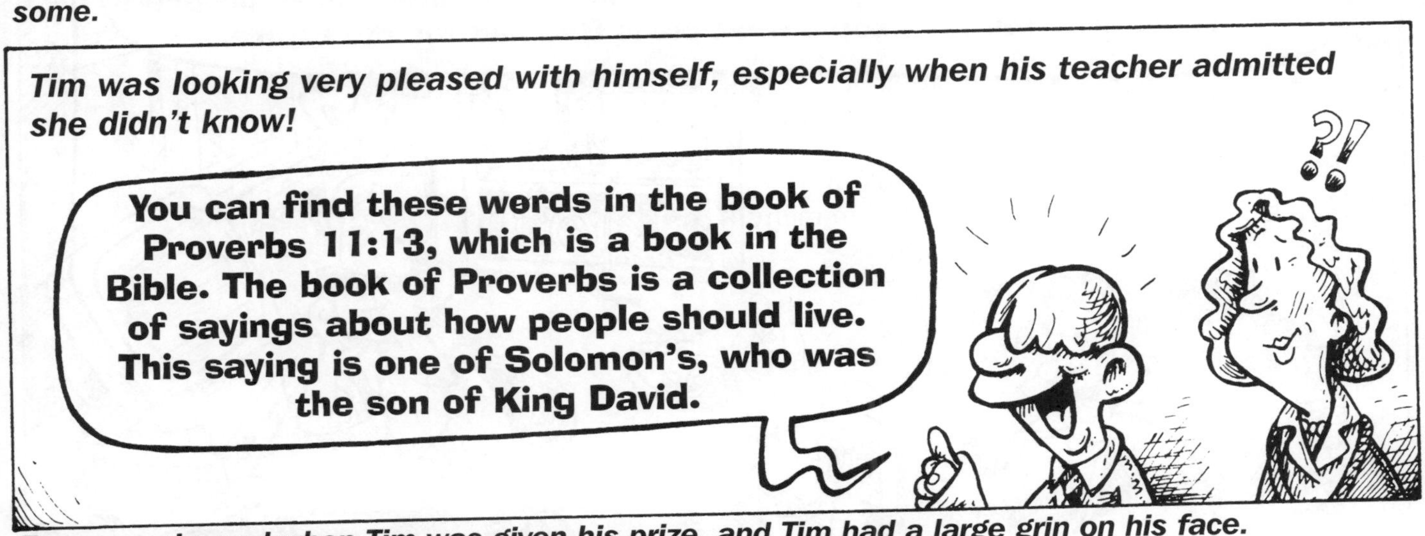
Tim was looking very pleased with himself, especially when his teacher admitted she didn't know!
You can find these words in the book of Proverbs 11:13, which is a book in the Bible. The book of Proverbs is a collection of sayings about how people should live. This saying is one of Solomon's, who was the son of King David.

Everyone clapped when Tim was given his prize, and Tim had a large grin on his face. 'Finding out about the Bible is great!' he thought.

Here are some proverbs from the book of Proverbs.
Can you match the two halves together correctly?

Sensible people accept	**Proverbs 10:8**	**you will be helped**
It is foolish to enjoy	**Proverbs 10:23**	**care of their animals**
Help others and	**Proverbs 11:25**	**doing wrong**
Sensible people always	**Proverbs 13:16**	**good advice**
Good people take	**Proverbs 12:10**	**think before they act**

If you have a Bible you could look them up to see which proverb goes with which reference.

You might be able to think of some more—or you could even try making up some of your own.

Back in Annie-log's bedroom, she and Little Ben had written up notes ready to report to the others and were getting ready for their next task. This was going to be gi-normous—the prophets. Boot had given her the names of all the prophets. There were 17 altogether. Too many to learn off by heart, they decided, so they wrote the names down to read to everyone.

Some of the names were strange and hard to say—Isaiah, Jeremiah, Lamentations, Ezekiel, Daniel, Hosea, Joel, Amos, Obadiah, Jonah, Micah, Nahum, Habakkuk, Zephaniah, Haggai, Zechariah and Malachi.

Obi-doo-dah,
Mickey,
Huggy...

Annie-log decided to use Boot to find information on the prophets.
She read from his factfile.

These books contain important messages that God wanted his special leaders, called prophets, to give to his people. Sometimes these prophets could even tell the people what plans God had for the future.
Hebrews 1:1
In the past, God spoke to our ancestors many times and in many ways through the prophets.

The prophets often used picture language to help the people to remember their promise to God, and to help them understand what God is like.

It is easy to forget what you have promised, isn't it?
Yes, I often need reminding of the things I should be doing. I think it would be helpful to have a picture to remind me.

Little Ben started drawing a cross with a heart around it. He told Annie-log that it helped him remember that Jesus loved him.

Annie-log drew a sheep with a shepherd's crook because it reminded her that Jesus looks after us like a shepherd.

Have you made your next 17 boxes? Cover them with paper and write the name of a prophet on each of the boxes. You could colour each of the sections a different colour to help you remember them.

Annie-log was wondering what sort of picture language the prophets used to tell people about what God is like. Thankfully, Boot came to the rescue. They looked at his screen and saw a row of pictures.

Annie-log saw how God can help enemies become friends.
Little Ben looked at the picture of a potter's wheel and realized that, just as the potter makes a good pot out of a lump of clay, so God can make us the best we can be if we put ourselves in his hands.
ISAIAH 11
JEREMIAH 18
EZEKIEL 37
ISAIAH 40:11
As they looked at the picture of dry bones from Ezekiel, they saw how dead everything was without God, and how we need God to make us truly alive.
Then they looked at a picture of God taking care of his flocks like a shepherd, carrying the lambs in his arms and gently leading their mothers in.

Annie-log's eyes grew wide with wonder. 'Why, that's my picture of Jesus,' she said.
What picture would you draw to best describe what God is like?

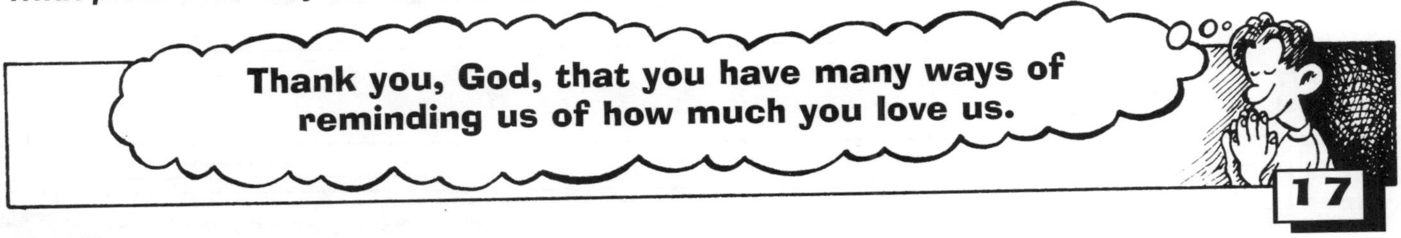
Thank you, God, that you have many ways of reminding us of how much you love us.

F A C T F I L E

The Livewires were all back in Annie-log's bedroom, reporting on their findings. They had all had a great time during the week and were very excited by all their discoveries. They typed all their information into Boot.

Can you help them fill in the factfile?

Books in the Old Testament ____________________

Sections in the Old Testament ____________________

First book in the Bible ____________________

King who wrote some of the Psalms ____________________

Can you find any of the books of the Old Testament in the wordsearch? You can look back over the last few days to remind yourself of their names.

D	E	U	T	E	R	O	N	O	M	Y	E	J	O	E	L
P	X	C	L	J	U	R	U	B	A	C	D	O	E	Z	E
N	O	G	I	H	T	I	M	J	K	L	S	S	S	R	V
U	D	R	S	Q	H	P	B	O	N	M	M	H	T	A	I
M	U	S	A	M	O	S	E	Z	L	Y	Z	U	H	E	T
B	S	T	I	U	V	W	R	A	D	C	B	A	E	A	I
E	H	I	A	G	J	E	S	G	N	I	K	R	R	S	C
R	M	L	H	K	F	P	Q	S	E	G	D	U	J	T	U
S	O	P	J	M	I	C	A	H	G	E	N	E	S	I	S
N	F	P	R	O	V	E	R	B	S	D	A	N	I	E	L
A	E	G	O	Z	B	Y	X	W	J	O	N	A	H	V	U
J	L	A	M	E	N	T	A	T	I	O	N	S	A	C	U

The Livewires made a huge poster of all the things they had discovered about the Old Testament. They agreed it had been fun and that they had learnt lots of new things. It had been an interesting Book Week. Annie-log turned Boot off... but when she looked again, he was still on! She tried again, and again and again!! They couldn't understand what was happening. Boot would not turn off! Suddenly, as they were looking at the screen, a message appeared on it.

JOHN 21:25
Now, there are many other things that Jesus did. If they were all written down one by one, I suppose that the whole world could not hold the books that would be written.
Gosh! Imagine all those books—I wouldn't run out of things to read.
We'd have to have Book Week every week—that would be great!
We could do our own Book Week and find out about some of the things Jesus did, couldn't we?

The Livewires thought this was a brilliant idea and wanted to get to work straight away. They decided to ask Boot a number of questions in order to get some information. Annie-log asked Boot, 'Where do we find all the stories of Jesus?'

They waited a minute or two before the answer came up on the factfile.

WEN ETASTNMTE HET RUFO GLOPSES
OK, clever clogs—another puzzle for us.

Can you work out the answer?

N_ _

T_ _ _ _ _ _ _ _

T_ _

F_ _ _

G _ _ _ _ _ _

New Testament The Four Gospels

Right, now we know where to start. Who's got the next question?

Little Ben, who loved reading and discovering new books, typed in the next question:

He thought he would like to write books when he grew up and was always keen to find out about authors.

Who wrote the New Testament?

The answer was soon on Boot's factfile.

Like the Old Testament, the New Testament was written by many different people, over many years. What we read in the New Testament was written after Jesus' life on the earth. Some of the writers had been friends of Jesus while he was alive, others became Christians later on.

While they were thinking about this, there was a knock at the door. It was Dave, their youth leader. He'd called to see how they had got on with their Book Week. They excitedly told him all about it and how they were carrying on their own Book Week to find out about the New Testament.

Dave picked up Quartz's Bible and read...

John 20:31: These things are written that you may believe that Jesus is the Messiah, the Son of God, and that through your faith in him you may have life.

Dave explained that although John wrote this about the gospel he had written, it could be true of all the New Testament. He told them that the New Testament starts with the gospels, which contain stories about the life of Jesus. Other books in the New Testament tell us how the Christian church spread after the death and resurrection of Jesus.

So you see, it is no ordinary book. If we read it carefully it will help us know Jesus better.

On a piece of paper, design a cover that you think would be good for the New Testament.

Help me, Father God, as I read about Jesus, to get to know him better.

After Dave had left them they were eager to find out more. Annie-log keyed into Boot again to look at all the books in the New Testament. They had quite a heated discussion about which books they were going to find out about next, and who was doing what! Eventually they decided to take the first five books. Apart from Little Ben, who was with Tim, they chose a book each. They left Annie-log to find out about Matthew. She decided she needed Boot's help as it was quite a big task, and typed in 'GOSPEL—MATTHEW'.

MATTHEW 9:9

Jesus left that place, and as he walked along, he saw a tax collector, named Matthew, sitting in his office. He said to him, 'Follow me.' Matthew got up and followed him.

Annie-log wondered if Matthew the tax collector was the same Matthew who had written Matthew's Gospel. She keyed into Boot again to find out some more facts, but Boot decided to have a little game with her. He didn't just give her the facts—she had to work for them! Can you see what he has done?

M_TTH_W W_S _ J_W
H_ W_RK_D F_R TH_ R_M_NS
M_TTH_W B_C_M_ _ FR__ND
_F J_S_S

Boot has missed out all the vowels—A E I O U. Can you put them in to see what he says about Matthew?

Annie-log decided that she had better find out what Matthew's book was about. She got her Bible out and began to look through the Gospel of Matthew. She read the story of the birth of Jesus and the men from the east who visited him. She remembered that they are often called the three kings or wise men. She did like that story—it reminded her that Christmas wasn't far away. As she read, she noticed that Matthew kept mentioning what the prophets had said. She sat quietly thinking about the way God had given the people pictures to remind them of him. And now here was Matthew telling us that their God had come to earth as a living person...

Dear Lord God, thank you for sending Jesus to show us what you are like.

There was so much in Matthew's book that she knew she needed Boot's help, so she wrote a few questions for him to answer. Here are the questions, with the answers—but Boot has got them all mixed up! Annie-log has had to match up the correct questions and answers. Can you follow the arrows to find the answers? If you've got a Bible you could look up the passages.

1. **Who does Matthew write about in his gospel?**
   1:1

2. **What happened to Jesus after he was baptized?**
   4:1

3. **Who were the four fishermen who became disciples of Jesus?**
   4:18–21

4. **What did Jesus do in the boat during the storm?**
   8:24

5. **How many loaves and fish did Jesus feed lots of people with?**
   14:17

6. **Who tried to walk on the water with Jesus?**
   14:29

7. **Which disciple betrayed Jesus with a kiss?**
   26:49

8. **How many times did Peter deny Jesus?**
   26:69–75

9. **How did Jesus die?**
   27:31

10. **What did Mary find when she visited the tomb of Jesus?**
    28:1–7

a) **Peter**

b) **He was crucified**

c) **Jesus**

d) **He went to sleep**

e) **He was tempted by the devil**

f) **Jesus had risen from the dead**

g) **Simon, Andrew, James and John**

h) **Five loaves and two fish**

i) **Judas**

j) **Three**

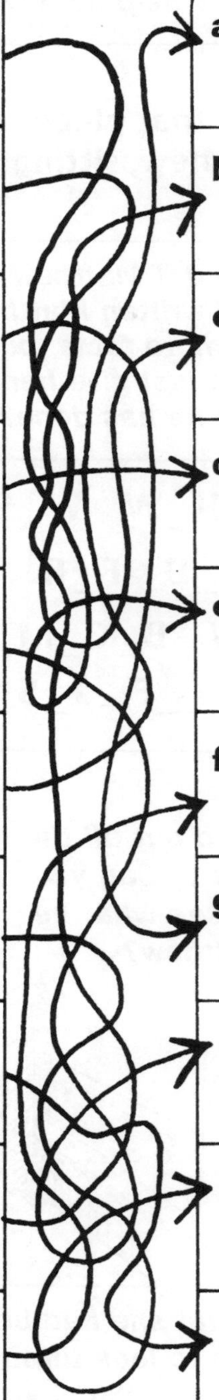

Annie-log looked back over all she had learnt and wondered if the others would find out as much as she had. She felt quite pleased, especially when she saw what Boot had written.

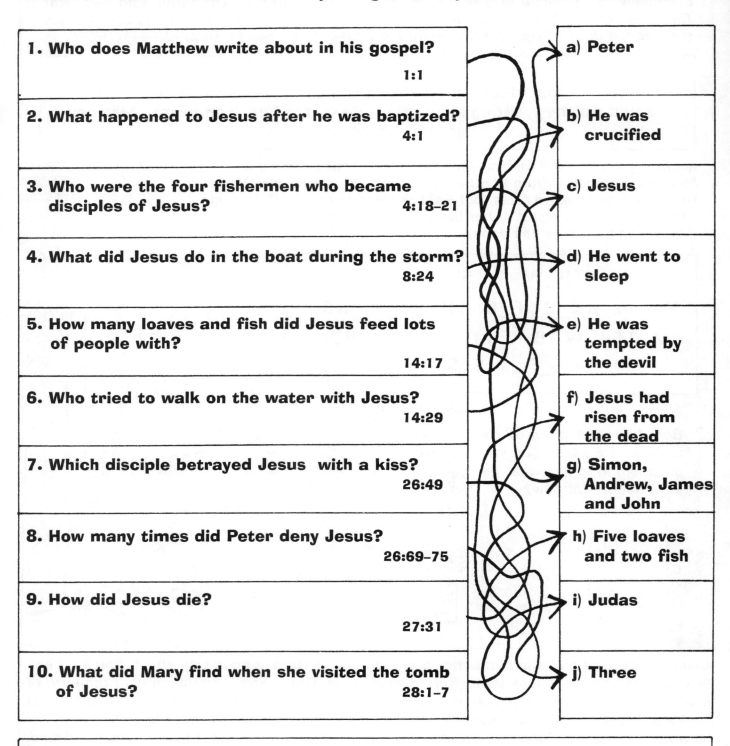

MATTHEW 19:14

Jesus said, 'Let the children come to me and do not stop them, because the kingdom of heaven belongs to such as these.'

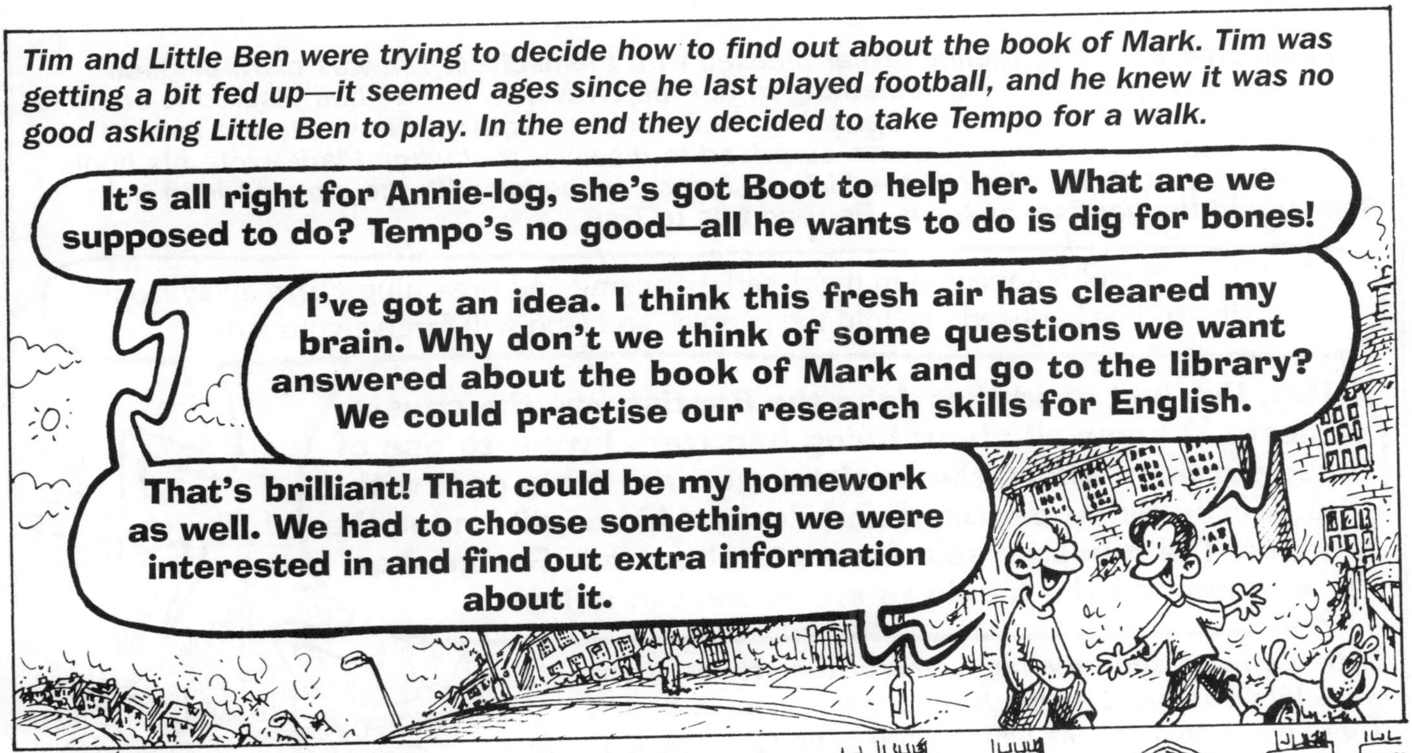
Tim and Little Ben were trying to decide how to find out about the book of Mark. Tim was getting a bit fed up—it seemed ages since he last played football, and he knew it was no good asking Little Ben to play. In the end they decided to take Tempo for a walk.
It's all right for Annie-log, she's got Boot to help her. What are we supposed to do? Tempo's no good—all he wants to do is dig for bones!
I've got an idea. I think this fresh air has cleared my brain. Why don't we think of some questions we want answered about the book of Mark and go to the library? We could practise our research skills for English.
That's brilliant! That could be my homework as well. We had to choose something we were interested in and find out extra information about it.

At the library Tempo was not very pleased because the librarian wouldn't let him in. He went to sleep outside, dreaming of bones!
LIBRARY

Inside, Tim and Little Ben found some books and quickly started reading. Tim wanted to get home to watch a football match on television. He almost shouted out loud when he found the answers to two of his questions.
Listen to this, Little Ben. They think that Mark was the first gospel to be written and it was probably written about 60 years after Jesus was born. It is thought that John Mark wrote it. Mark is the shortest gospel and tells the story of Jesus' life.
Tim read out the first verse of Mark.
Mark 1:1: This is the Good News about Jesus Christ, the Son of God.

Why do you think it is Good News about Jesus? Complete the sentence:

I think Jesus is Good News because ....

....

....

Tim and Little Ben were feeling rather pleased with themselves. Tim was extra pleased because not only did he have something to tell the Livewires, but he had also done some of his homework. Now it was Little Ben's turn to find out something. He wanted to know a little bit about some stories. He was surprised to discover that when Mark wrote his book, he didn't start with the story of the birth of Jesus—he began with the story of John the Baptist and the baptism of Jesus. He read this to Tim.

Mark 1:4: So John appeared in the desert, baptizing and preaching. 'Turn away from your sins and be baptized,' he told the people, 'and God will forgive your sins.'

Hey, I've just read that John the Baptist was the cousin of Jesus. I know all about being baptized. I went to one of those services where the minister got into a big pool with the person being baptized and ducked him right under the water. The minister said it was to show that God makes us clean on the inside when we believe in him.

Little Ben was soon reading some of the stories. There were lots of stories about Jesus making people better. There were also stories which were called parables. These were good, but you had to concentrate because there was usually a special meaning that Jesus wanted the people to understand.

Little Ben was enjoying reading about the time when Jesus fell asleep in the boat and there was a huge storm. The disciples were afraid they were going to die so they woke Jesus up. It was getting really exciting...

Listen to this, Tim. Guess what Jesus did?
Mark 4:39: Jesus stood up and commanded the wind, 'Be quiet!' and he said to the waves, 'Be still!' The wind died down, and there was a great calm.

Feeling excited and pleased, they both set off for home. Tempo was delighted to see them again and ran in and out of their legs, wagging his tail like mad!

Can you see which way Tim and Little Ben went to get home?

Time was running out and Quartz was getting more and more stuck. She'd asked her mum and dad if they knew anything about Luke. They had got a few books to look at, but they weren't really any good. In the end she decided to call Dave on the telephone and explain her problem. Dave was very happy to help and invited her to his house. She quickly hurried round. What a surprise she had when she arrived—there, eating chocolate biscuits, were Data and Digit!

Hi, you two. Are you stuck too?
Yep! We were going round and round in circles so in the end we decided to get help.
Dave gave Quartz some biscuits and asked which books they were trying to find out about.
I'm Luke.
I'm John.
And I'm the Acts of the Apostles! But I don't even know who they are!!
Right then, let's make a start with Luke. Actually, there's a link here because most people think that Luke, who wrote the Gospel of Luke, also wrote Acts. He was a doctor, you know.
Dave then read out his favourite verses from Luke—12:6 and 7:
Aren't five sparrows sold for two pennies? Yet not one sparrow is forgotten by God. Even the hairs of your head have been counted. So do not be afraid; you are worth much more than many sparrows!
That's a nice verse. I can understand why you like it. It means that God knows us and cares for us whoever we are, doesn't it?
That's right. Perhaps we could all say a prayer thanking God for his love and care.

Quartz, Digit and Data were getting very interested in what Dave was saying.
Do we know anything else about Luke, apart from his being a doctor?
Well, yes we do. We know he spoke Greek and he also went with Paul on some of his journeys.
Quartz wanted to know what other stories were in Luke, so Dave gave them each a Bible and they had to find out for themselves. Quartz liked reading the story of the shepherds visiting the baby Jesus just after he had been born.
Imagine sitting quietly with your sheep one night and being visited by all those angels. I bet they had the fright of their lives! But they were really pleased they went, weren't they?
Digit liked the story of the man who was let down through the roof by his friends. He couldn't walk but Jesus made him better. Data liked reading the story of the shepherd searching for one lost sheep and being happy and excited when he found it, just like God is happy when we turn to him.
Look! Here's the prayer we say at church and school. I didn't know it was in the Bible. Jesus taught it to his disciples.
After reading quietly for some time, Quartz read out the prayer.
Luke 11:2–4: Jesus said to them, 'When you pray, say this: "Father: May your holy name be honoured; may your kingdom come. Give us day by day the food we need. Forgive us our sins, for we forgive everyone who does us wrong. And do not bring us to hard testing."'

Make a bookmark out of card. Write the words of this special prayer on it and decorate it.

Quartz was now happy—she had enough to report back to the other Livewires. She stayed with Digit and Data while they found out about their books.
Right then, it's my turn now. I'm doing the Gospel of John. I expect it's like the other gospels, isn't it?
Well actually, no. It's very different from Matthew, Mark and Luke.
Trust me to get the different one! I knew mine would be the hardest! So what is so different about this gospel?
OK, are you ready? John's Gospel was the last gospel to be written. He probably wrote it about 90 years after the birth of Jesus. When John wrote this gospel, he wasn't too concerned about telling people the facts about the life of Jesus, but he wanted them to understand who Jesus really was—the Son of God. He does this by writing about the meaning of what happened.
Hold on a moment, you've lost me! What do you mean by the meaning?
Dave then told them the story of Jesus changing the water into wine when he was at a wedding. The wine had run out, and Jesus told the servants to fill six large stone jars with water. When the master of the house tasted it, it was very good wine. Dave then read this verse:
John 2:11: Jesus performed this miracle in Cana in Galilee: there he revealed his glory, and his disciples believed him.
Right... I think I'm beginning to understand. He didn't just change the water into wine because he could do things like that—it was to help people see that he was a pretty special person—the Son of God?
Got it!

You could make the next four books for your Bible library. Write the names of each of the gospels on the sides.

After hearing the story of the wedding, the Livewires started talking about weddings they'd been to. Data and Digit weren't too keen on them. There were too many boring bits like speeches and photographs. Quartz liked them, particularly if there was good food, music and dancing! Dave interrupted their chatter to remind them what they were supposed to be doing.

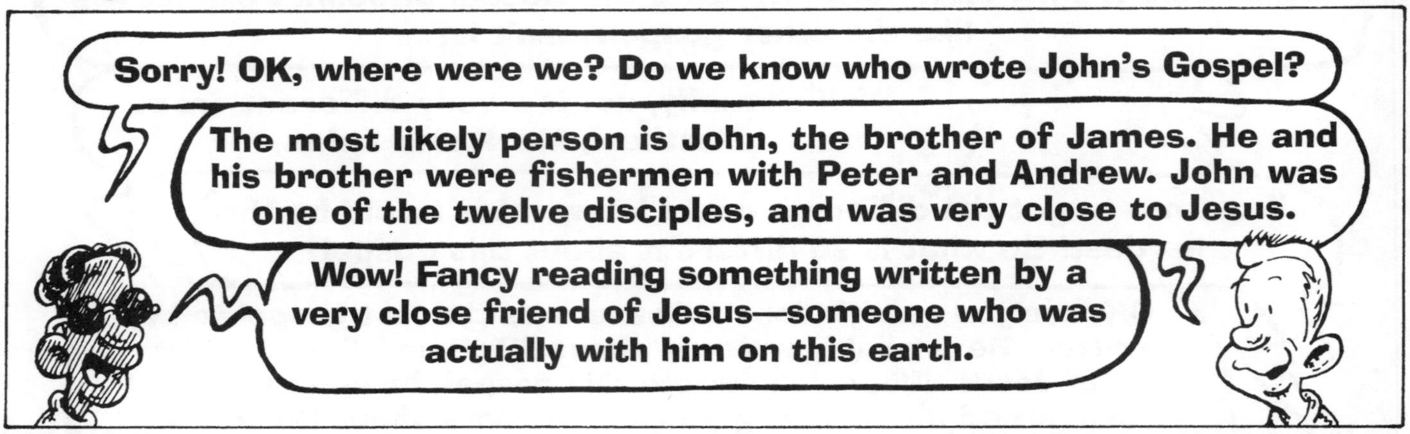
Sorry! OK, where were we? Do we know who wrote John's Gospel?
The most likely person is John, the brother of James. He and his brother were fishermen with Peter and Andrew. John was one of the twelve disciples, and was very close to Jesus.
Wow! Fancy reading something written by a very close friend of Jesus—someone who was actually with him on this earth.

Dave told them that there were seven well-known sayings in John's Gospel called the 'I am' sayings. They are called this because Jesus describes himself in seven different ways, saying, 'I am...'. Dave read one of the descriptions to help the Livewires understand.

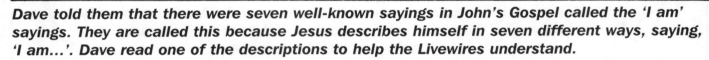

John 8:12: Jesus said, 'I am the light of the world. Whoever follows me will have the light of life and will never walk in darkness.'

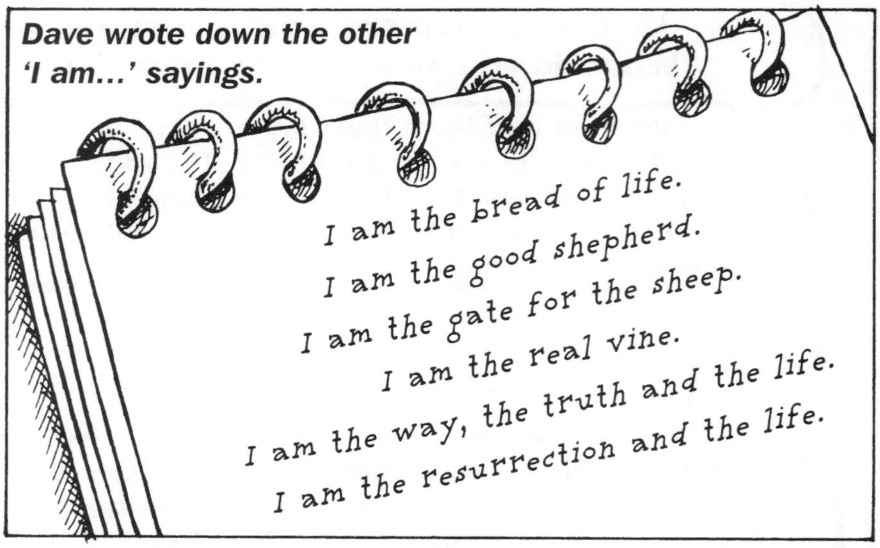
Dave wrote down the other 'I am...' sayings.
I am the bread of life.
I am the good shepherd.
I am the gate for the sheep.
I am the real vine.
I am the way, the truth and the life.
I am the resurrection and the life.

With Dave's help, the Livewires matched up the meanings with the sayings. Can you work out which saying goes with which meaning? You'll need your Bible for this!

1. Bread

2. Shepherd

3. Gate

4. Vine

5. Way, truth and life

6. Resurrection and life

7. Light

Jesus keeps us close to him.

Jesus is the signpost to God.

Jesus makes it possible for us to live with him for ever.

Jesus shows us the truth.

Jesus looks after us.

Jesus keeps us in God's fold.

Jesus helps us grow as Christians.

You will need to look up these verses in John's Gospel: 14:6, 6:48, 10:9, 8:12, 10:14, 11:25, 15:5.

Dave was very impressed with their ideas but decided it was time to move on to look at Acts.

Now, from what I can remember, Acts isn't like the gospels, is it? The apostles were Jesus' chosen followers, weren't they?
That's right. Acts tells the story of how the Christian church spread and is mainly about the adventures of people like Peter and the other apostles. And Paul—we'll find out more about him later on. Do you remember who wrote it?
You said it was Luke, didn't you? The same person who wrote the Gospel of Luke.
That's right. Acts tells how the Holy Spirit was sent to the apostles after Jesus had gone back to be with his Father. They had some good times when they met and shared meals in each other's homes. Lots of people became followers of Jesus.
Sounds like they may have had some good parties!
It wasn't all fun. Some people didn't like what Peter and John were preaching. They were arrested, but it didn't stop them telling others about Jesus. Listen to this.
Acts 5:29: Peter and the other apostles replied, 'We must obey God, not men.'

Dave told them that some people were so angry about what the apostles were teaching that they stoned them. Stephen was actually stoned to death because he told others about Jesus.

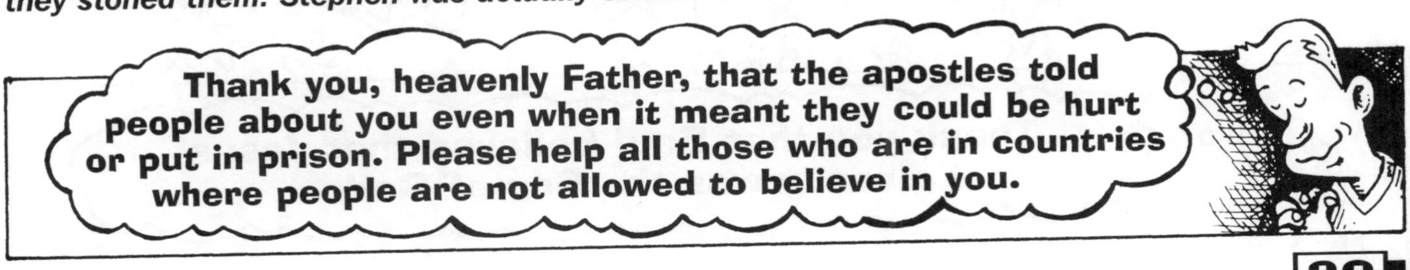
Thank you, heavenly Father, that the apostles told people about you even when it meant they could be hurt or put in prison. Please help all those who are in countries where people are not allowed to believe in you.

Quartz, Digit and Data wanted to know why the people at the time didn't want to hear about Jesus. Dave told them that some of the Jewish people did not believe that Jesus really was the Son of God because they had been expecting a different sort of person, one who would be more like a king and, with his army, fight the Romans who were ruling them. These people thought that those who believed in Jesus as the Son of God were going to upset their way of life and just make things even more difficult.

But it didn't stop the apostles telling others about Jesus, did it, or we wouldn't know about him today?
That's a very good thought, Data. No, it didn't stop them, even though they knew they could be thrown into prison or even killed like Stephen. Luke tells of some wonderful ways in which God helped them. Some of those who didn't like the new Christians became believers themselves.

Dave told them how Saul, who was one of the Jewish leaders, had tried hard to destroy the new church. Then he met with Jesus in a vision on the road to Damascus, when he was on his way to arrest more Christians. Saul was blinded and he heard Jesus speaking to him.

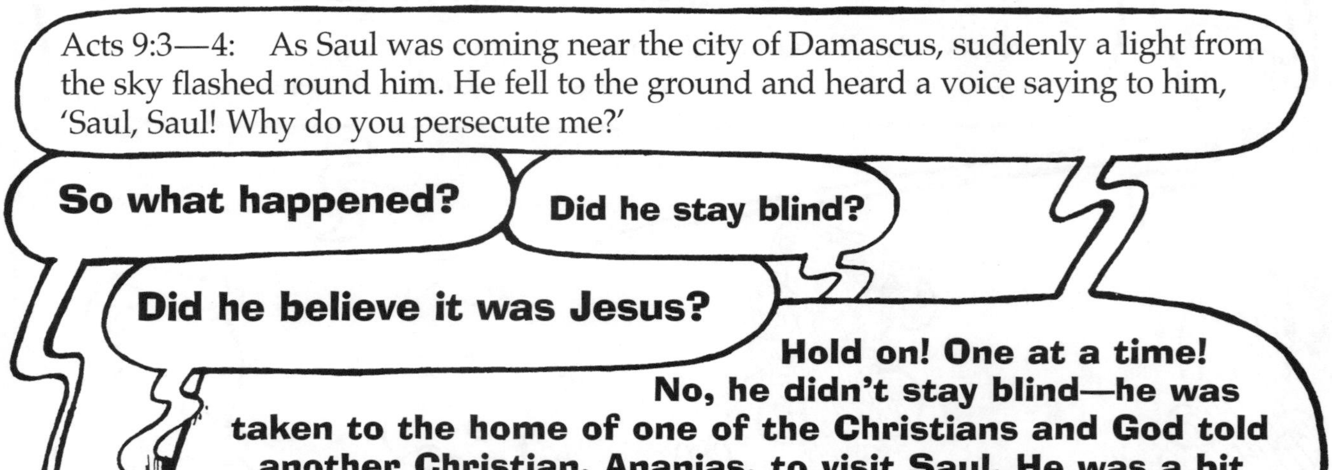

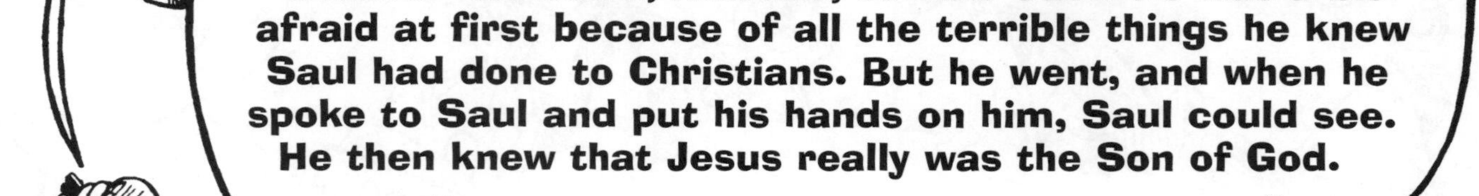

To continue your Bible library, label one of the boxes 'Acts'.

F A C T F I L E

To help you remember some of the things you have read about, the Livewires have made up this word puzzle for you. If you have a Bible you may find it helpful to look up some of the stories.

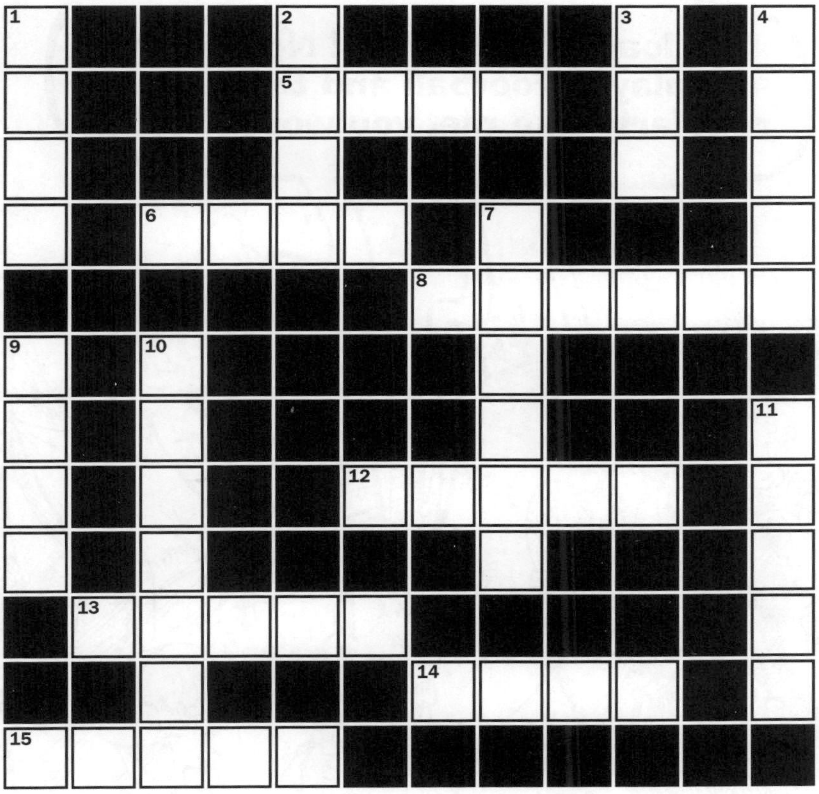

C L U E S

Across

5. Luke wrote this book and a gospel.
6. The stories of the birth of Jesus are in the Gospels of Matthew and ____.
8. What profession was Luke?
12. In John 6:35, Jesus said, 'I am the _____ of Life.'
13. The story of the Lost _____ is in Matthew 18:12–14 and Luke 15:4–7.
14. In the Gospel of ____ we can find the seven 'I am' sayings of Jesus.
15. The story of the _____ is in Matthew 13:1–9, Mark 4:3–9 and Luke 8:4–8.

Down

1. In Matthew 19:16–24 and Mark 10:17–25, Jesus told the ____ man that it was easier for a camel to go through the eye of a needle than for a ____ man to enter the kingdom of God.
2. ____ begins his gospel with the story of John the Baptist.
3. In Luke 2:41–52 we read how the ___ Jesus stayed in the temple talking to the teachers.
4. Jesus turned the _____ into wine at a wedding—John 2:1–12.
7. ______ means 'Good News'.
9. In Matthew 14 and Mark 6 we can read about Jesus feeding the ____ thousand.
10. In the gospel of _______ you can read about the wise men from the east visiting Jesus.
11. We read how Jesus calmed the _____ in Matthew 8:23–27 and Luke 8:22–25.

The Livewires had just completed a long walk. They were with a lot of their friends on a week's holiday with their youth group. During the day they were doing lots of different activities, and sleeping in tents each night.

They more or less got their tents tidy and enjoyed their supper of jacket potatoes, beans and sausages. Now they were sitting around the campfire, singing. Soon Dave started telling them the exciting story of how Saul became a follower of Jesus. The Livewires remembered how this happened from doing their extra bit of work on Book Week. Do you remember where Saul met Jesus? They were really pleased when they could answer the questions.

Sometimes we have to do things we're not keen on doing, and may even be a bit afraid of doing. Ananias was chosen by God to go and visit Saul after he had been blinded. Why do you think he was afraid?
Acts 9:13: Ananias answered, 'Lord, many people have told me about this man and about all ... . he has done to your ...... in Jerusalem.'

Dave told the group that Ananias did go and visit Saul, and God used him to let Saul see again.

Have you ever been afraid of doing something, but then it has turned out OK? Think about what you did and then say this prayer:

Dear Lord, Thank you for helping me when I had to...

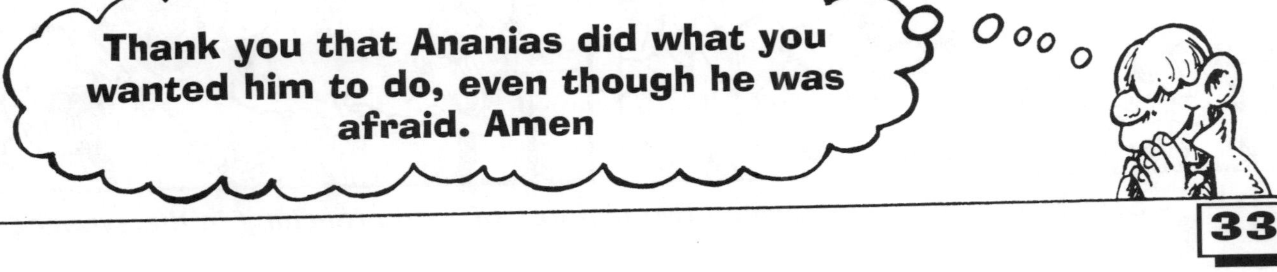
Thank you that Ananias did what you wanted him to do, even though he was afraid. Amen
Oooo

The Livewires and the others in the group had all admitted being afraid of doing something. Little Ben had been afraid to own up to breaking his mum's cup, and Annie-log had been afraid when she first went in a canoe. Data told them how afraid she had been when she and her family got lost when they were out walking.

They were busy talking to each other when Dave asked for a bit of quiet. He asked them whether they thought it was easy to change the way we behave and to start doing things differently.

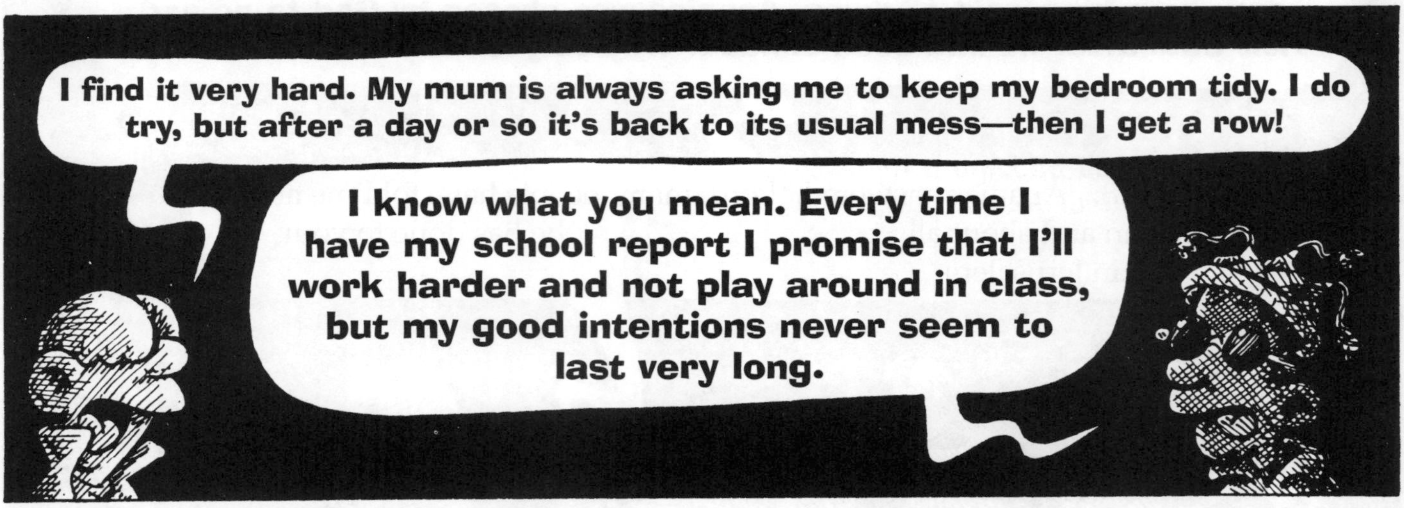
I find it very hard. My mum is always asking me to keep my bedroom tidy. I do try, but after a day or so it's back to its usual mess—then I get a row!
I know what you mean. Every time I have my school report I promise that I'll work harder and not play around in class, but my good intentions never seem to last very long.

Dave asked them how they thought Saul would change after what happened to him on the road to Damascus. This time Quartz took the Bible from Dave and read out...

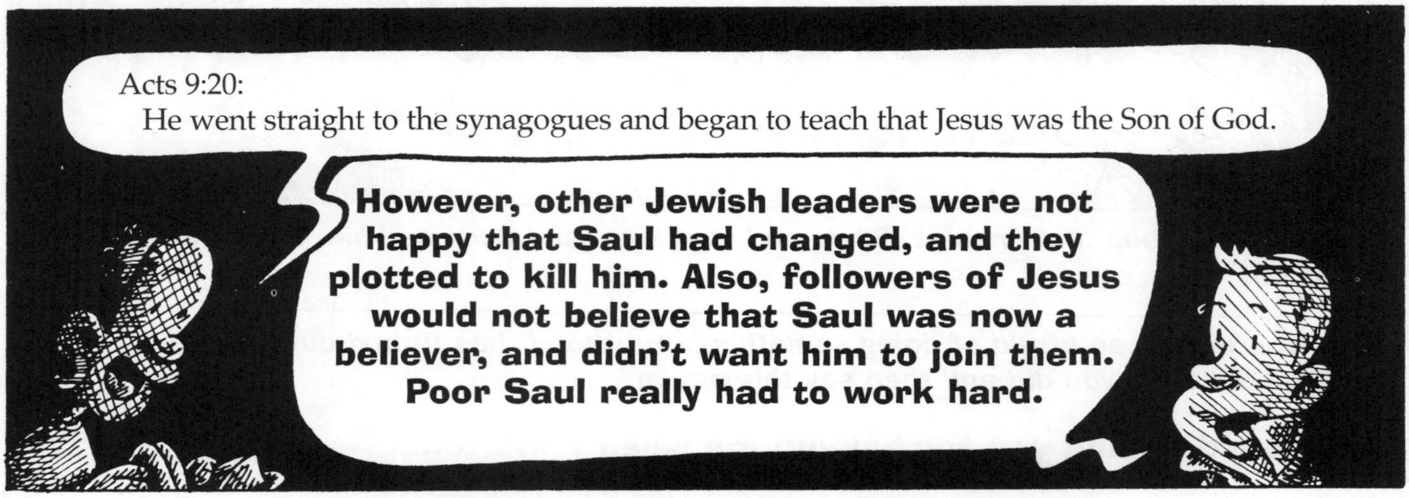
Acts 9:20:
He went straight to the synagogues and began to teach that Jesus was the Son of God.
However, other Jewish leaders were not happy that Saul had changed, and they plotted to kill him. Also, followers of Jesus would not believe that Saul was now a believer, and didn't want him to join them. Poor Saul really had to work hard.

Everyone could remember a time when being a Christian had not been easy.

Can you?

Spot the differences between two pictures of Saul preaching in the synagogues.

The Livewires were trudging up a steep hill in the sunshine. Their rucksacks contained lunch, snacks and drinks. Everyone was feeling tired as no one had got much sleep during the night.

Tim missed Tempo, and was hoping that his mum would remember to take him for walks. Quartz didn't know how she would manage without her radio or Walkman.
You lot sound like a load of moaning minnies. Cheer up! We're going to stop for lunch soon.

While they were lazing around after lunch, Dave reminded them of the story of Saul. He told them that after he had become a follower of Jesus, Saul went on journeys to tell people living in other countries about Jesus.

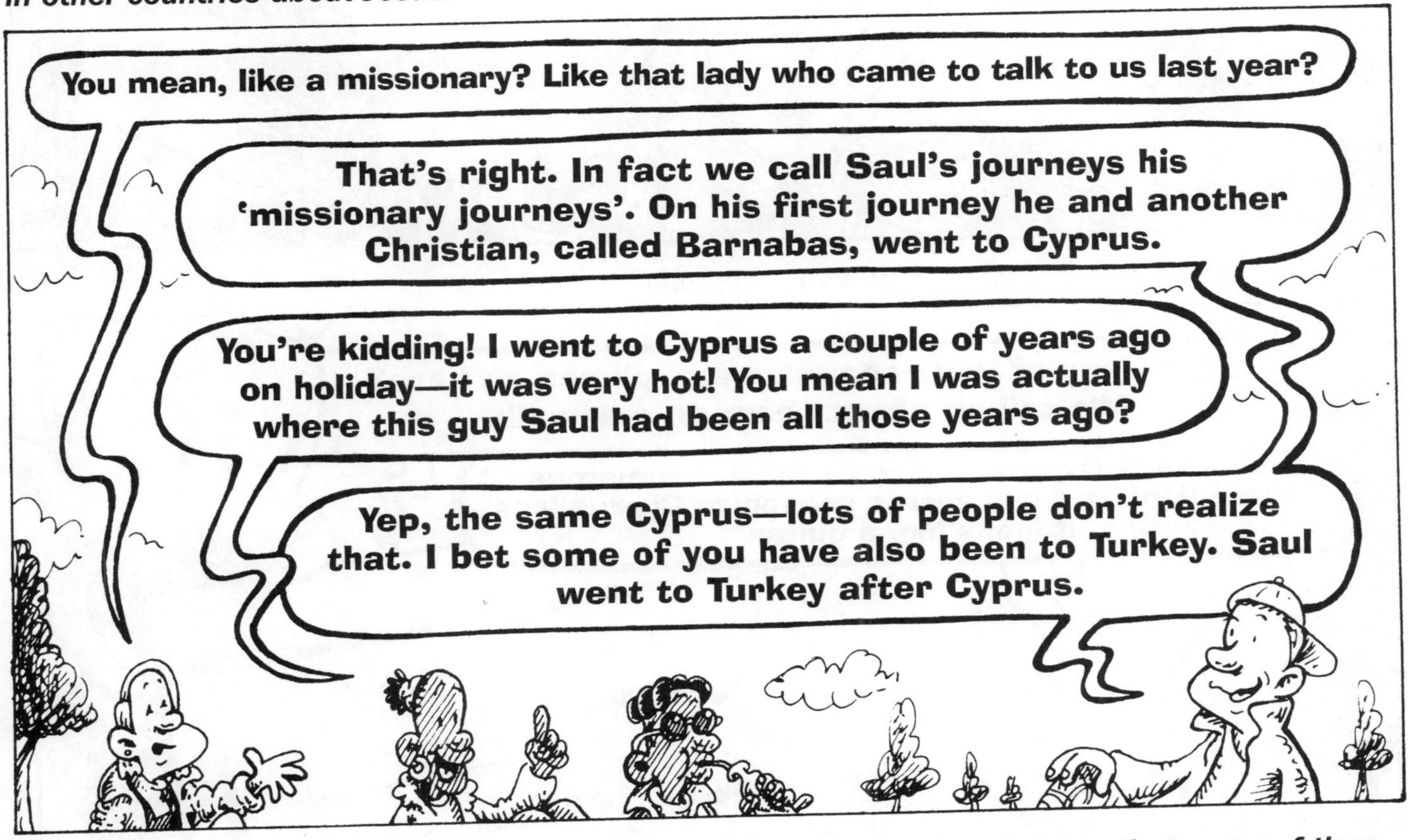
You mean, like a missionary? Like that lady who came to talk to us last year?
That's right. In fact we call Saul's journeys his 'missionary journeys'. On his first journey he and another Christian, called Barnabas, went to Cyprus.
You're kidding! I went to Cyprus a couple of years ago on holiday—it was very hot! You mean I was actually where this guy Saul had been all those years ago?
Yep, the same Cyprus—lots of people don't realize that. I bet some of you have also been to Turkey. Saul went to Turkey after Cyprus.

They were amazed to learn that these people had been to the same places that some of them had visited. Dave told them that a lot of people became believers as a result of Saul's teaching. Annie-log took the Bible and, with Dave's help, found the right place, and read out...

Acts 13:43: After the people had left the meeting, Paul and Barnabas were followed by many Jews and by many Gentiles who had been converted to Judaism. The apostles spoke to them and encouraged them to keep on living in the grace of God.

Thank you, Father God, for all those who go to other countries to tell people about Jesus. Please look after them. Amen

Later that evening, after supper, everyone was sitting around the campfire again.

Just then, Dave came out of his tent with a big map.

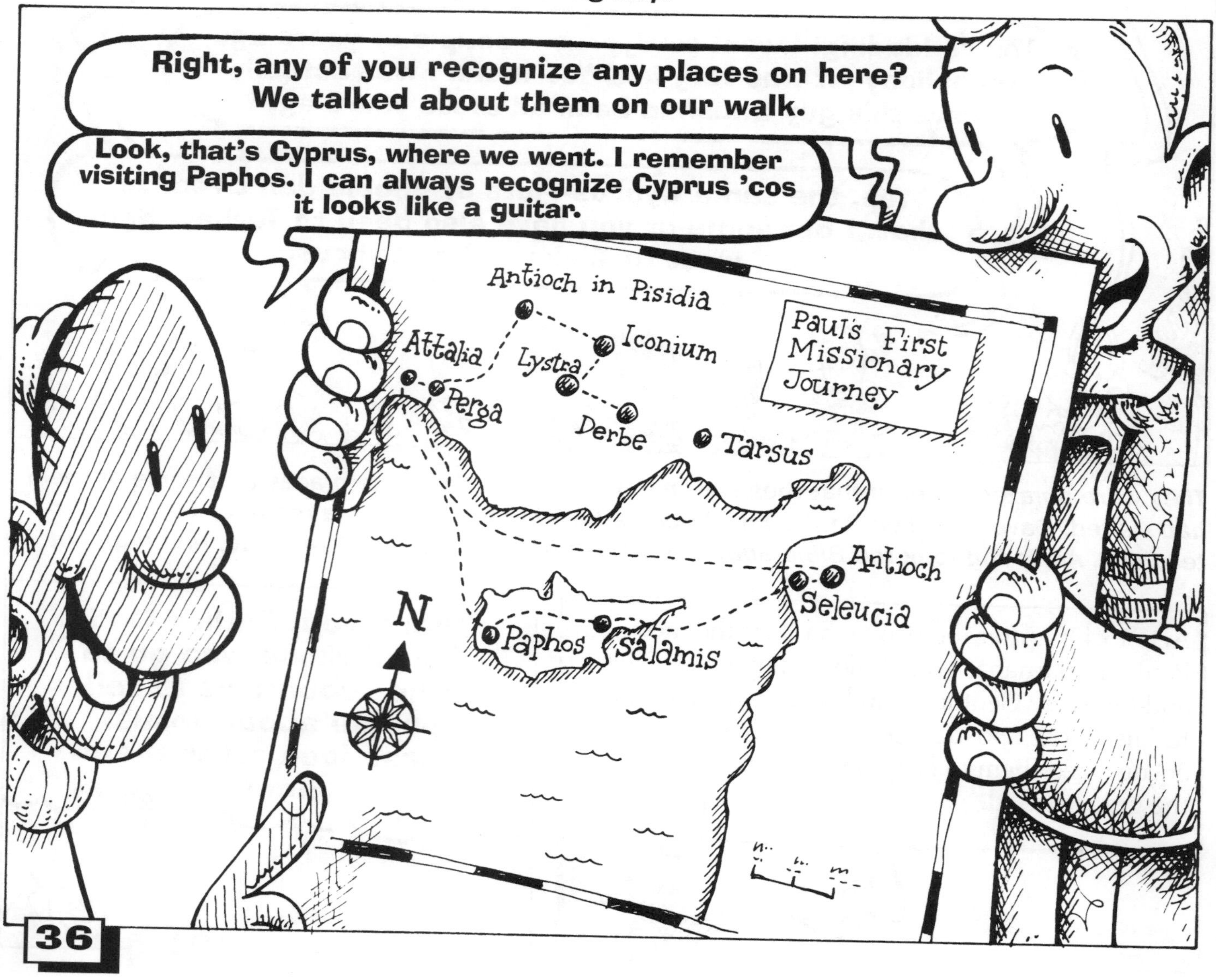

Dave showed them the places that Saul and Barnabas visited on that journey. He had an atlas with the names of the places as they are known today. Perhaps you can find an atlas and look too. Tim wanted to know if everybody accepted what Saul and Barnabas said to them.
BIG WORLD ATLAS

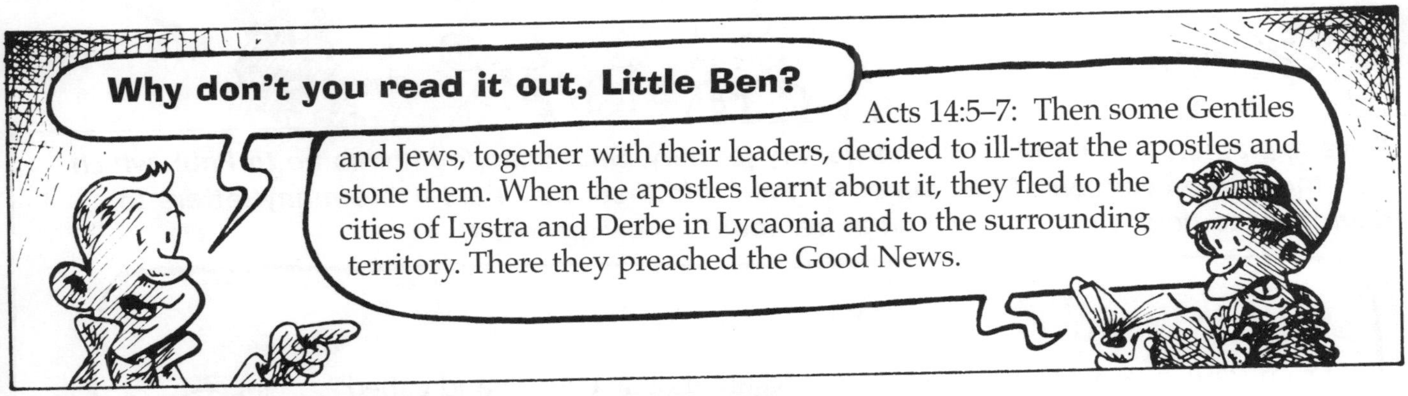
Why don't you read it out, Little Ben?
Acts 14:5–7: Then some Gentiles and Jews, together with their leaders, decided to ill-treat the apostles and stone them. When the apostles learnt about it, they fled to the cities of Lystra and Derbe in Lycaonia and to the surrounding territory. There they preached the Good News.

Little Ben paused for a minute before saying anything...

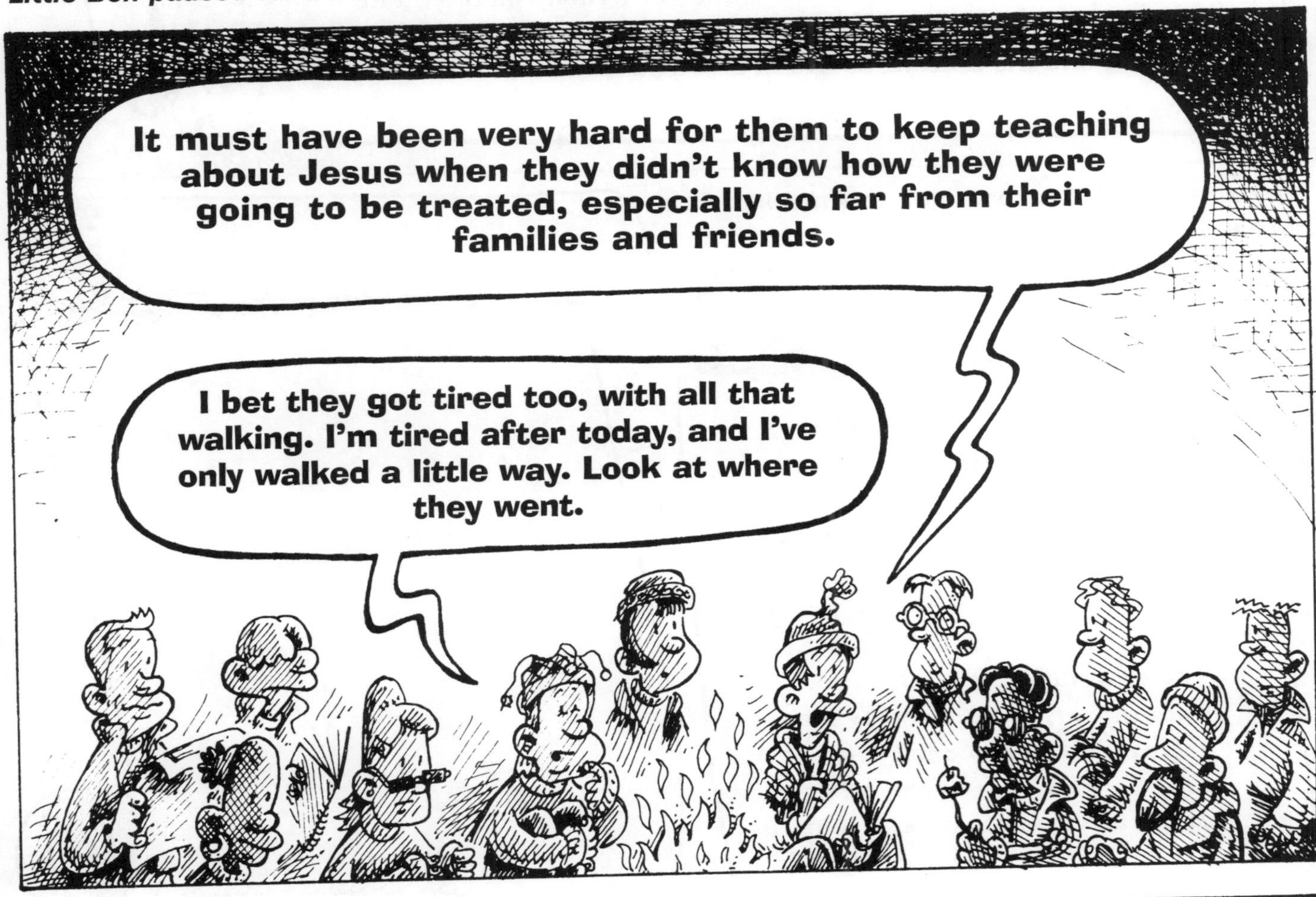
It must have been very hard for them to keep teaching about Jesus when they didn't know how they were going to be treated, especially so far from their families and friends.
I bet they got tired too, with all that walking. I'm tired after today, and I've only walked a little way. Look at where they went.

Colour in the map. Shade the sea in blue and the land in green. How do you think they travelled on their journey?

It was another sunny day and the Livewires were lazing in the sun with everybody else. They had just returned from a super swim. Dave asked them all to start writing letters home to let their families know they were all OK and enjoying themselves. They all sat there, chewing pens and looking at blank pieces of paper. No one knew what to write! Dave came up with an idea.

Why not write the letter like Paul wrote his letters to the churches?
That's a great idea. By the way, are Saul and Paul the same person?

Dave explained that on his first missionary journey, Saul changed his name to Paul, which was the Roman version of his name. He then told them that Paul wrote many letters to churches, to help them understand more about following Jesus.

Romans 1:1 and 7:

From Paul, a servant of Christ Jesus and an apostle chosen and called by God to preach his Good News… And so I write to all of you in Rome whom God loves and has called to be his own people: May God our Father and the Lord Jesus Christ give you grace and peace.

They all thought it a good idea to write like Paul.
Here is Data's letter:

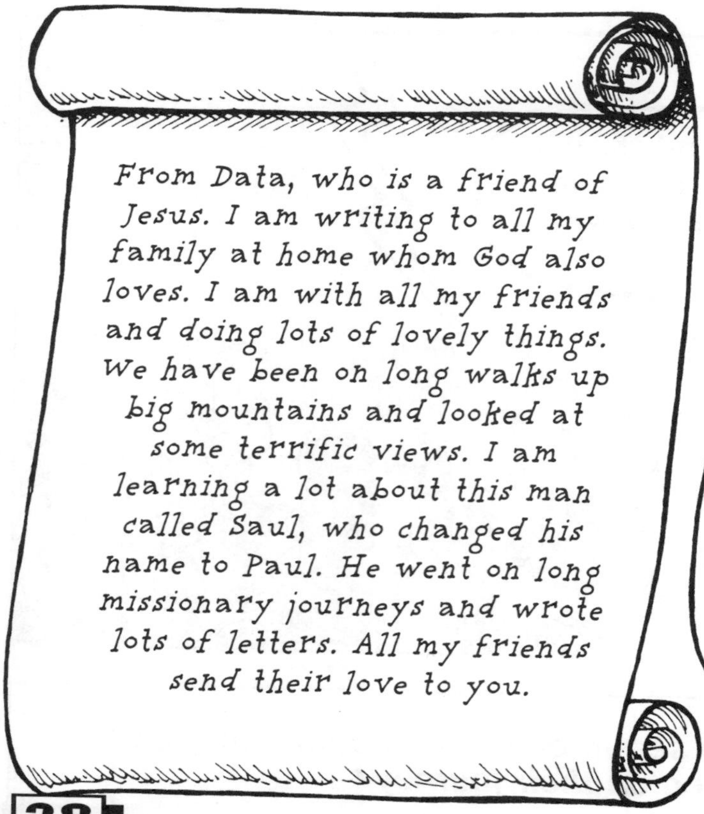
From Data, who is a friend of Jesus. I am writing to all my family at home whom God also loves. I am with all my friends and doing lots of lovely things. We have been on long walks up big mountains and looked at some terrific views. I am learning a lot about this man called Saul, who changed his name to Paul. He went on long missionary journeys and wrote lots of letters. All my friends send their love to you.

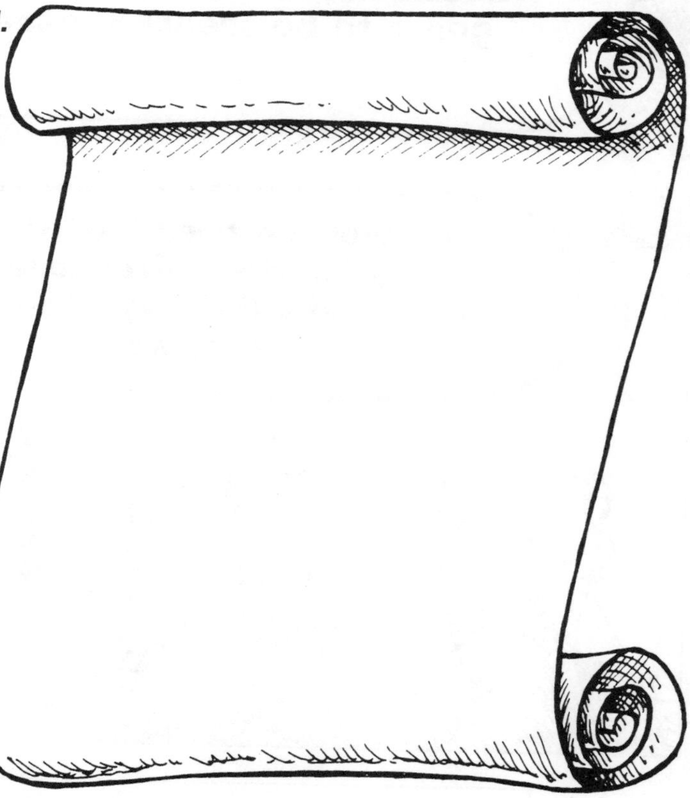

Imagine you are at camp with the Livewires. What would your letter home say?

Later that evening, everyone was recovering from their afternoon activities. They had done abseiling, rock climbing and canoeing.

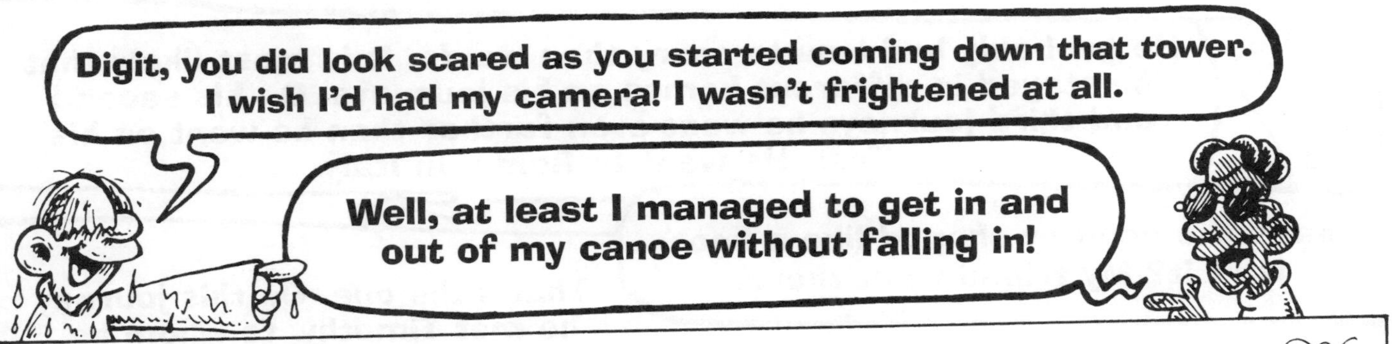
Digit, you did look scared as you started coming down that tower. I wish I'd had my camera! I wasn't frightened at all.
Well, at least I managed to get in and out of my canoe without falling in!

Everyone laughed at the sight of Tim, dripping wet.
But I beat you to the top of the rock face, didn't I?
All right, you lot—enough of this silly squabbling. You all did very well. You sound just like the church at Corinth. Paul wrote to them because they were quarrelling with one another about how things should be done and what exactly they should believe. Listen to what Paul said to them:

1 Corinthians 13:4–7:

Love is patient and kind; it is not jealous or conceited or proud; love is not ill-mannered or selfish or irritable; love does not keep a record of wrongs; love is not happy with evil, but is happy with the truth. Love never gives up; and its faith, hope and patience never fail.

Tim and Digit felt ashamed of themselves when they heard that. Dave explained that Paul wanted the Corinthians to realize that loving one another was very important.

Digit was busy scribbling a coded message on his pad. Can you work it out?

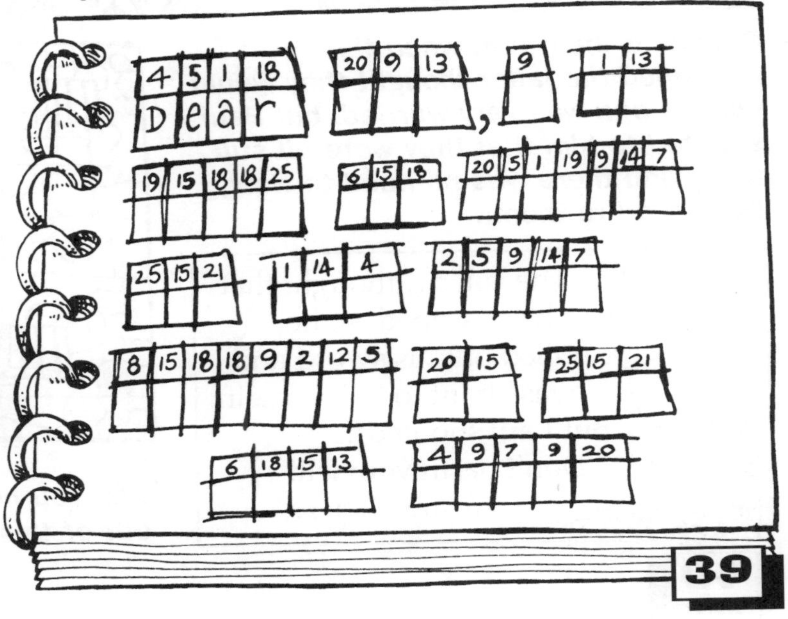

Early the next morning Dave woke everybody up—they had to pack up their tents and move on to the next campsite. They were trying to get everything fitted into rucksacks.

How far is it to the next site?
It's about 6 or 7 miles—we'll stop for lunch on the way.
Do you think Paul had to take all his stuff when he went on his missionary journeys? Did they have tents to carry as well?
He probably had less to carry than we do. It is most likely that he stayed in different homes on his journeys. On his second and third journeys he went even further than he went on his first. He went to Rome, in Italy.
That's the country shaped like a boot, isn't it? My friend went there.
That's the one. On this journey he met Timothy, to whom he wrote later. He also got thrown into prison with Silas, another follower of Jesus, because some people didn't like what they were doing. But even when they were in prison they still kept praising God. While they were singing, there was an earthquake and the prison doors opened and the chains fell off the prisoners.
Good! They were able to escape, then?
Holy BIBLE

Dave told them that when this happened the jailer thought they would escape and was very worried, but Paul shouted to him that they were all still there and there was no need to worry. Dave read to them…

Acts 16:28: The jailer… thought that the prisoners had escaped; so he pulled out his sword and was about to kill himself. But Paul shouted… 'Don't harm yourself! We are all here.'

Can you help Paul and his friends find their way out of this prison maze?

Having arrived at the new camp and set up the tents, Dave organized a wide game before supper. He got everybody into teams and explained that there were coloured envelopes hidden around the field and in the woods. He placed a map for each team in the middle of the field. The first challenge was to fill in all the places where Paul went on his second and third missionary journeys by finding the envelopes which were the same colour as their map. The Livewires' map was blue. They set off...

I wish Tempo was with us—he'd soon nose out the clues.
Look! What's that over there?
And over there!

Soon everyone had a clue in their hand. They ran back to the map and opened their envelopes. Can you work out which clues fit?

ntioch
hesus
ilippi
essalonica
orinth
ystra
erusalem
iletus
yre

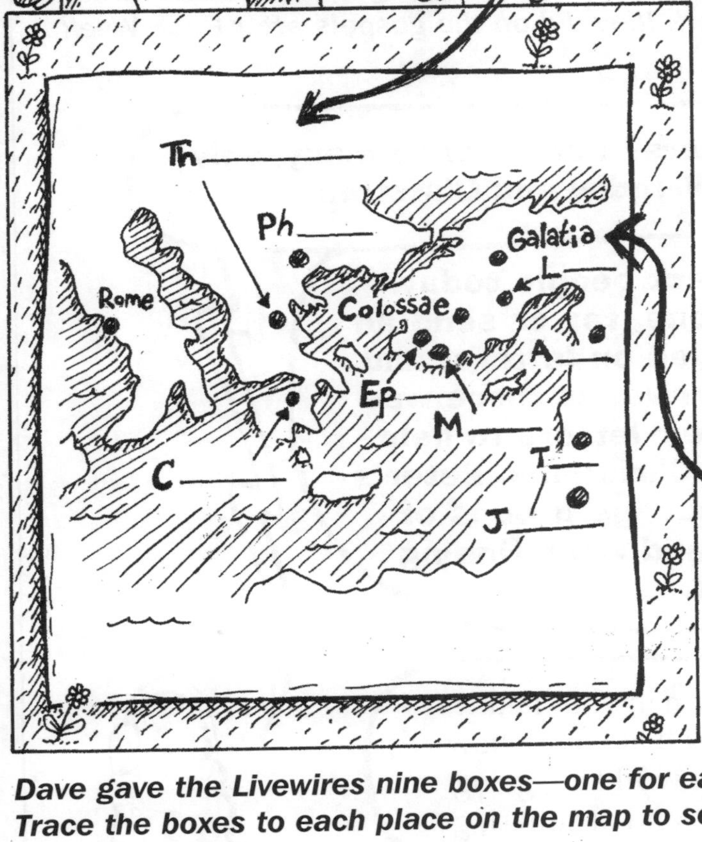

When their map was completed they ran up to Dave.

Well done, guys! Here's the next challenge...

Dave gave the Livewires nine boxes—one for each letter that Paul had written to the churches. Trace the boxes to each place on the map to see where each letter was sent.

The final challenge is to find out who took Paul's letter to the church at Colossae for him.

I'll get a Bible!

Quartz read out this verse...

Colossians 4:7 and 8:

Our dear brother Tychicus, who is a faithful worker and fellow-servant in the Lord's work, will give you all the news about me. That is why I am sending him to you, in order to cheer you up by telling you how all of us are getting on.

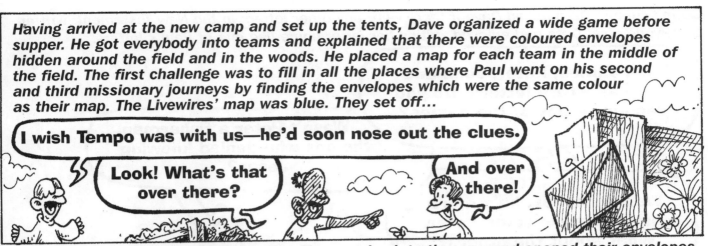

During supper, Data asked Dave if there were any other letters in the New Testament, written by anyone else. Data had enjoyed writing her letter home like one of Paul's letters.

Yes, James, Peter, John and Jude all wrote letters. Do you recognize any of the names?
Wasn't Peter a fisherman, the one who denied knowing Jesus?
Well done! Yes, he's more than likely the same Peter. What about the others?

They all had a few guesses, but no one really knew. Dave told them that James and Jude were brothers of Jesus, and John was the same man who wrote the gospel. The Livewires were cross they hadn't known that from the work they did on the gospels after Book Week.

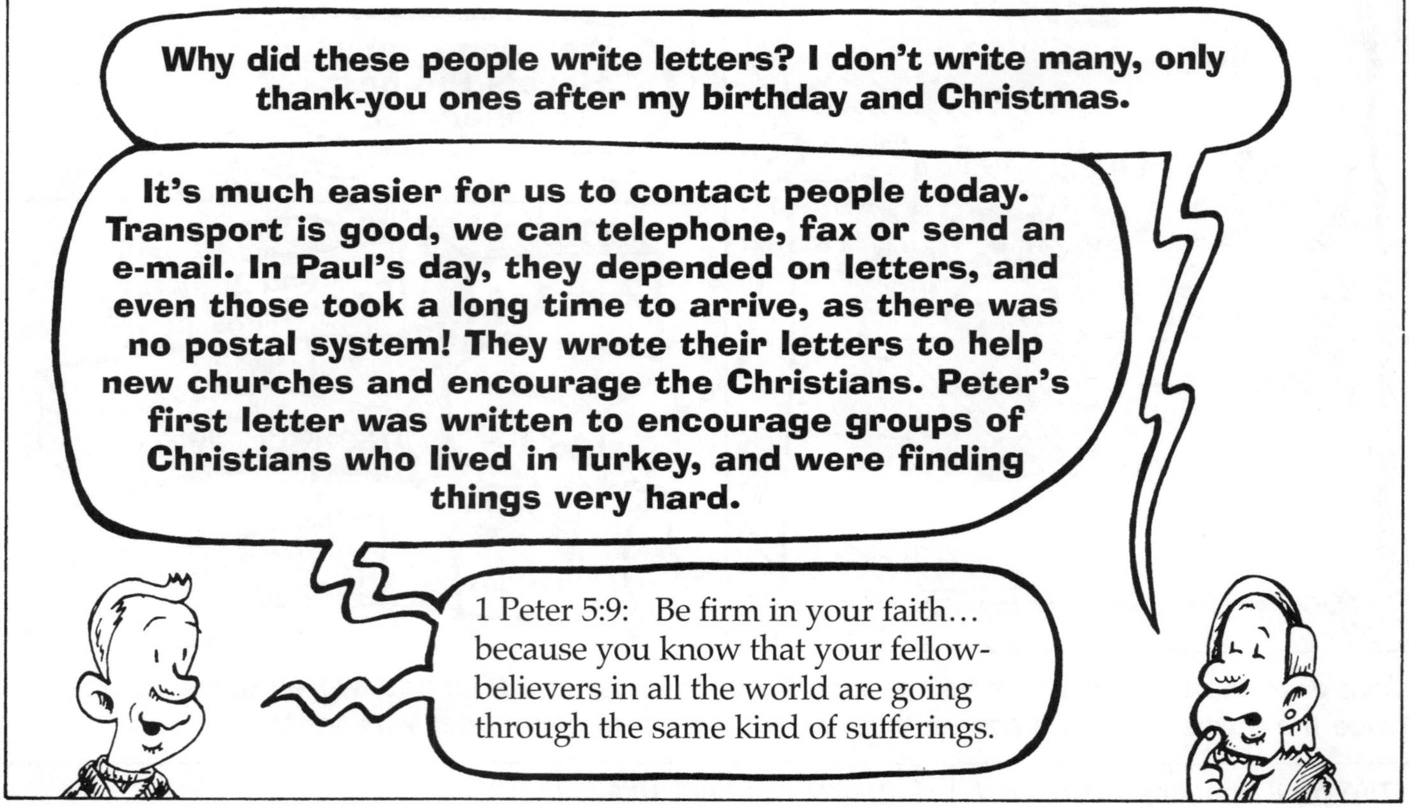
Why did these people write letters? I don't write many, only thank-you ones after my birthday and Christmas.
It's much easier for us to contact people today. Transport is good, we can telephone, fax or send an e-mail. In Paul's day, they depended on letters, and even those took a long time to arrive, as there was no postal system! They wrote their letters to help new churches and encourage the Christians. Peter's first letter was written to encourage groups of Christians who lived in Turkey, and were finding things very hard.
1 Peter 5:9: Be firm in your faith… because you know that your fellow-believers in all the world are going through the same kind of sufferings.

Dear Lord, please be with anyone who is finding it hard to be a Christian.

If you have been making your Bible library, you need to get busy on the rest of the New Testament—all the letters—21 altogether!! Let's do the letters Paul wrote to the churches today.

You will need to write these names on the boxes:

Romans, 1 Corinthians, 2 Corinthians, Galatians, Ephesians, Philippians, Colossians, 1 Thessalonians, 2 Thessalonians.

Dave began talking to them about what it was like being a Christian. Everyone agreed that at times it was hard. Many didn't like to tell friends they were Christians in case they laughed at them.

That's why it helps us when we meet together—we remember that we're not the only Christians. It sort of encourages us and helps us to be stronger.
The letters that Paul and the others wrote probably encouraged the early Christians. They weren't too sure what to believe. It was all quite new to them, and they had to cope with bullying and teasing because they were Christians. To receive a letter encouraging them to go on living as Christians must have been very important. Imagine reading this when you were a bit unsure of what you believed...
See how much the Father has loved us! His love is so great that we are called God's children—and so in fact we are.
That's really good. I often need to be reminded of that. Who wrote it?
See if you can work it out from these clues:
• He was very close to Jesus.
• He wrote a gospel.

Who do you think the mystery letter-writer might be?

You may know someone who is having a tough time at the moment. Perhaps you could write a short note to them, telling them you are thinking about them.

It's time to get some more books ready for our Bible library. We've almost finished! Today, let's do the letters written by Paul to individuals: 1 Timothy, 2 Timothy, Titus and Philemon. You could also do the letter to the Hebrews, but we don't know for certain who wrote it. Then you could do your boxes for the last lot of letters—those written by individuals other than Paul. You need to write on them: James, 1 Peter, 2 Peter, 1 John, 2 John, 3 John and Jude.

As the next day was their last day at camp, they spent it tidying things up so that they could make an early start in the morning. Although they didn't want to leave, they were looking forward to seeing their families again. After lunch Dave had promised them an exciting end to the week. They were going to learn all about the last book in the Bible—Revelation.

Soon everyone was sitting on the grass, waiting for Dave and the other leaders. When they arrived Dave gave everyone a piece of paper and a pencil. He asked them to sit quietly on their own for a few minutes and to think about their church. He asked them to think about all the good things about the church—the people, friends, clubs, services, songs and anything they liked about their church. There was silence for a long time as they chewed their pencils and thought.

Dave then asked them to draw pictures of all the things they had thought about. When they had finished, they exchanged papers with someone and they each had to work out from the pictures what the person liked about their church.

There was a lot of noise and shouts of excitement as they guessed correctly.

The book of Revelation has lots of pictures. They are pictures that God gave to John to share with the Christians. God gave him pictures of seven churches. Some things in the pictures are good, but some of them are not. This is what he says to the church at Ephesus...
Revelation 2:2, 4: I know what you have done; I know how hard you have worked and how patient you have been… But this is what I have against you: You do not love me now as you did at first.
I think that's true for me. I sometimes forget about loving Jesus. I need to remember it every day.

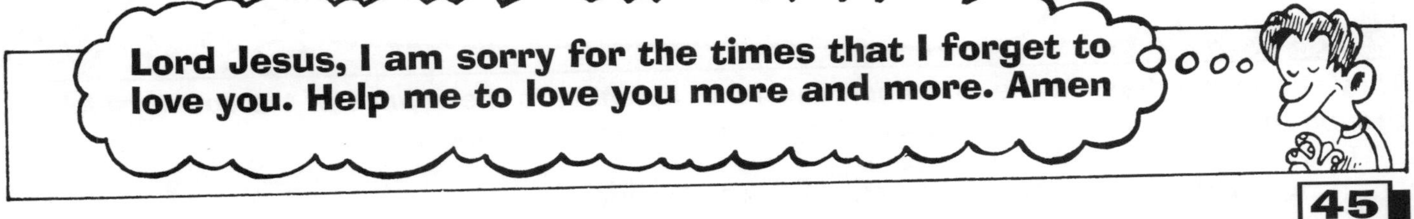
Lord Jesus, I am sorry for the times that I forget to love you. Help me to love you more and more. Amen

Everyone had really enjoyed using their imagination to draw their pictures so they were pleased when Dave gave them another piece of paper. This time, what they had to think about was much harder because no one had ever been there—they really did have to use their imagination! Dave asked them to think about heaven and what they thought it would be like! That set them thinking. You could almost see their thought bubbles!

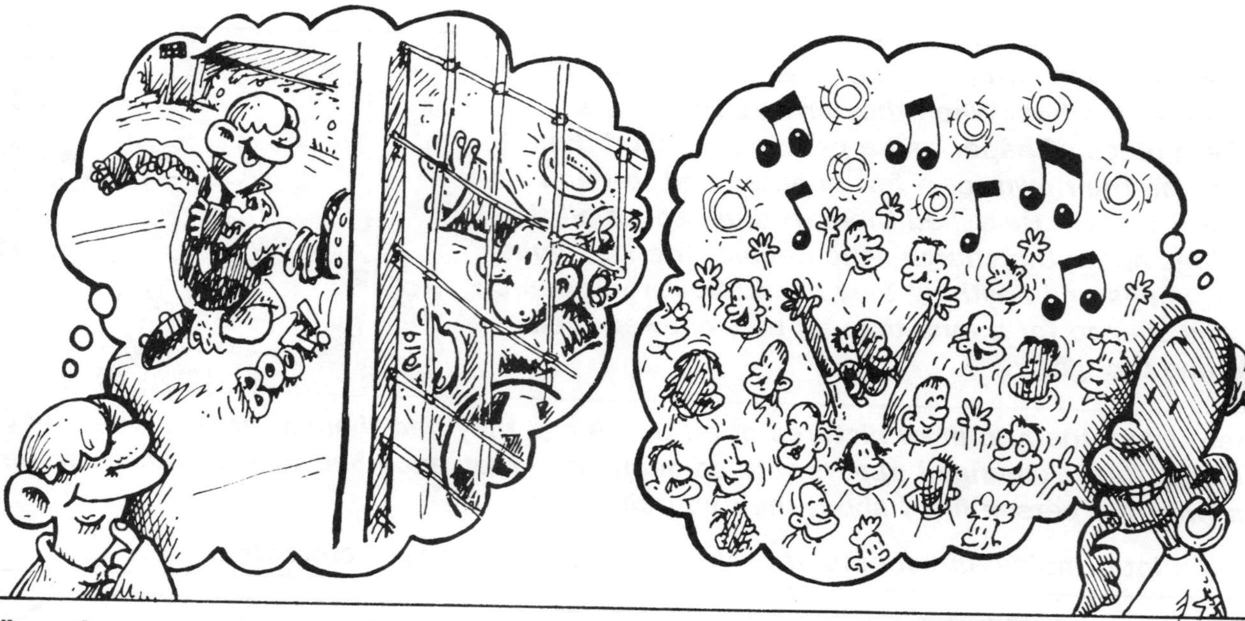

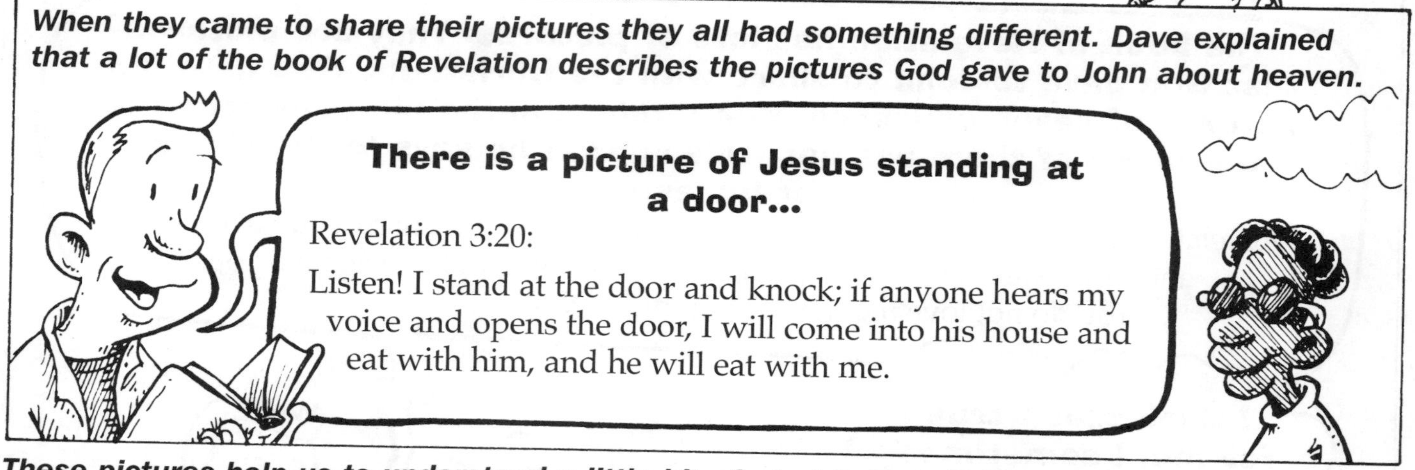

When they came to share their pictures they all had something different. Dave explained that a lot of the book of Revelation describes the pictures God gave to John about heaven.
There is a picture of Jesus standing at a door...
Revelation 3:20:
Listen! I stand at the door and knock; if anyone hears my voice and opens the door, I will come into his house and eat with him, and he will eat with me.

These pictures help us to understand a little bit of what heaven is like—but Paul tells us in one of his letters that no one really knows.

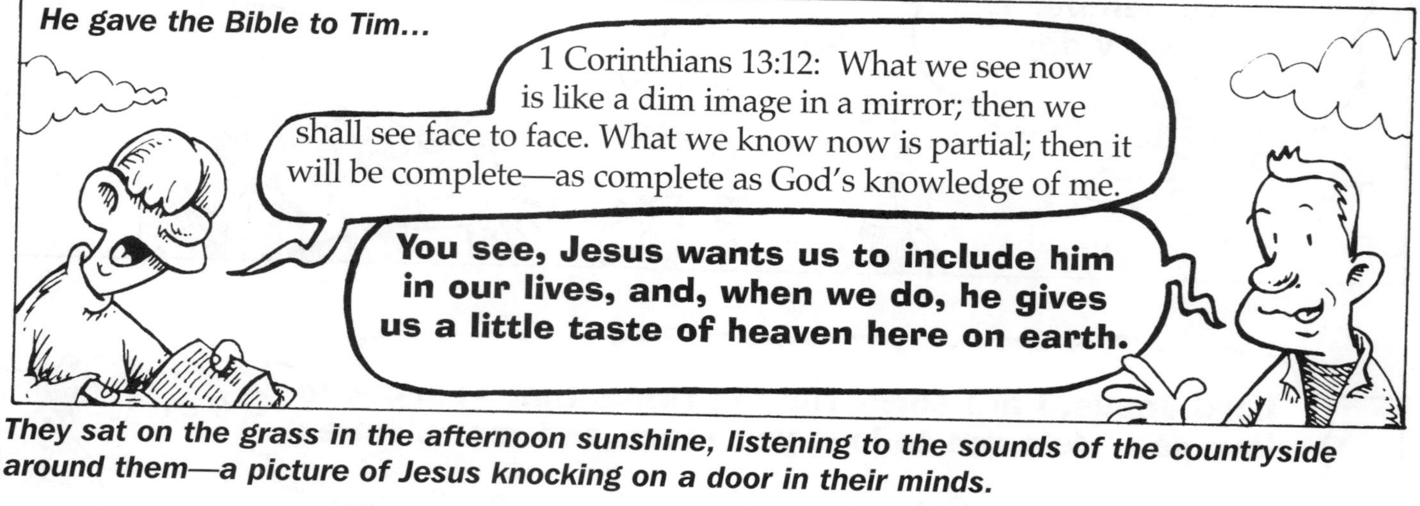

He gave the Bible to Tim...
1 Corinthians 13:12: What we see now is like a dim image in a mirror; then we shall see face to face. What we know now is partial; then it will be complete—as complete as God's knowledge of me.
You see, Jesus wants us to include him in our lives, and, when we do, he gives us a little taste of heaven here on earth.

They sat on the grass in the afternoon sunshine, listening to the sounds of the countryside around them—a picture of Jesus knocking on a door in their minds.

What is your picture of heaven like?

FACTFILE

You can now do your last book for your Bible library—Revelation. Well done for completing your library!

During the evening the Livewires made up a huge wordsearch to help them remember all they had learnt at camp.

B	C	R	C	Y	P	R	U	S	O	J	P	L	D
T	H	E	S	S	A	L	O	N	I	A	N	S	C
I	T	V	J	A	P	U	H	H	M	M	O	W	M
M	I	E	D	U	J	A	E	O	P	E	M	E	I
O	T	L	A	L	B	P	B	J	A	S	E	R	S
T	U	A	H	G	F	E	R	D	P	C	L	B	S
H	S	T	I	P	E	T	E	R	H	J	I	E	I
Y	M	I	S	T	C	A	W	L	O	K	H	H	O
N	R	O	M	A	N	S	S	Q	S	R	P	S	N
O	P	N	E	P	H	E	S	I	A	N	S	T	A
X	W	S	N	A	I	P	P	I	L	I	H	P	R
C	O	R	I	N	T	H	I	A	N	S	V	U	Y
Y	Z	A	B	S	N	A	I	S	S	O	L	O	C
F	G	G	A	L	A	T	I	A	N	S	C	D	E

Here are the clues for you to find the words:

1. A brother of Jesus who wrote a letter _ _ _ _ _
2. A younger brother of Jesus whose letter was quite short _ _ _ _
3. A fisherman who denied Jesus _ _ _ _ _
4. No one knows for certain who wrote this letter _ _ _ _ _ _ _
5. Paul wrote this letter to the church at Ephesus _ _ _ _ _ _ _ _ _
6. The people of Rome _ _ _ _ _ _
7. _ _ _ _ changed his name to _ _ _ _
8. Paul wrote a letter to him _ _ _ _ _ _ _
9. The people of Corinth _ _ _ _ _ _ _ _ _ _ _
10. The people of Philippi _ _ _ _ _ _ _ _ _ _ _
11. He wrote a gospel and three letters _ _ _ _
12. The last book of the Bible _ _ _ _ _ _ _ _ _ _
13. Paul went to this country _ _ _ _ _ _
14. Paul made a visit to this city _ _ _ _ _ _
15. Paul was a _ _ _ _ _ _ _ _ _ _
16. Paul wrote him a letter _ _ _ _ _ _ _ _
17. The people of Thessalonica _ _ _ _ _ _ _ _ _ _ _ _ _
18. The people of Colossae _ _ _ _ _ _ _ _ _ _
19. The people of Galatia _ _ _ _ _ _ _ _ _
20. Paul wrote a letter to him _ _ _ _ _
21. You can read about Paul's missionary journeys in this book _ _ _ _

Some time after the camp, the Livewires were once again at Annie-log's house. They were trying to think of something exciting to do during the half-term holiday coming up soon. While they were talking, Dave called round to see them. He had a favour to ask them.

I guessed you'd all be here. Are you doing anything special in the holidays?

Dave explained that he was running a holiday Bible club for younger children during that week, and he wanted the Livewires to help. As you can imagine, they were keen.

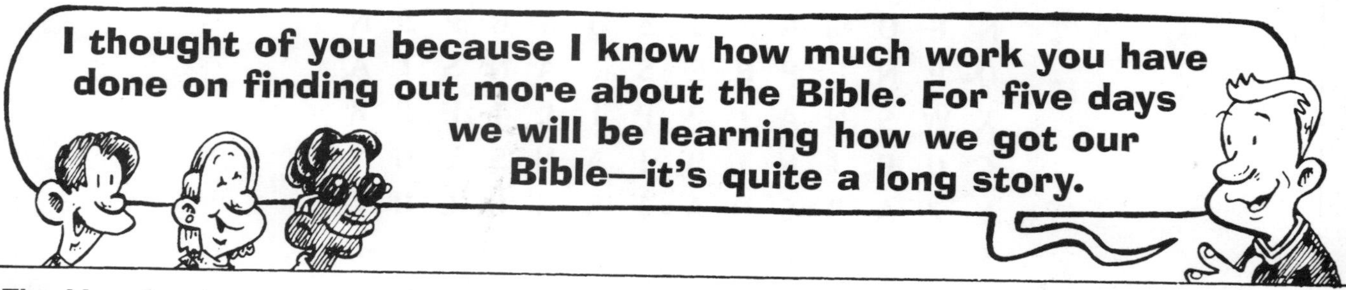
I thought of you because I know how much work you have done on finding out more about the Bible. For five days we will be learning how we got our Bible—it's quite a long story.

The Livewires were very excited. Dave gave them a few ideas about the sort of thing they would be looking at to help them get started. He told them that he also wanted to help the children understand how important the Bible is for us today even though parts of it were written a very long time ago. He read out something that Paul had written in his letter to Timothy...

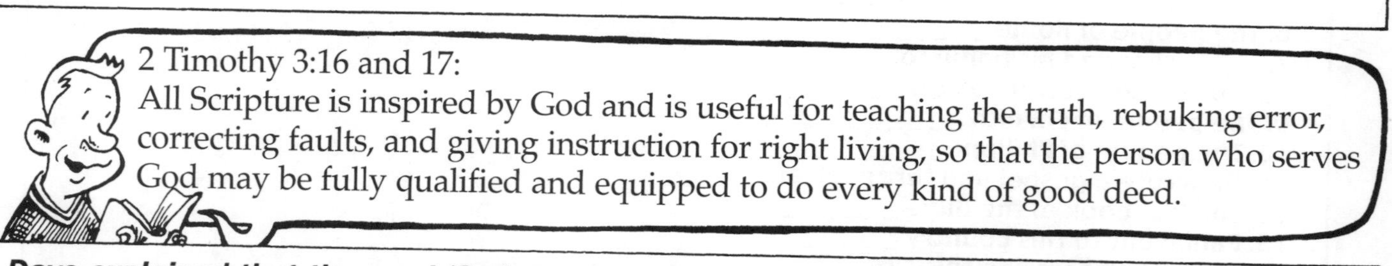
2 Timothy 3:16 and 17:
All Scripture is inspired by God and is useful for teaching the truth, rebuking error, correcting faults, and giving instruction for right living, so that the person who serves God may be fully qualified and equipped to do every kind of good deed.

Dave explained that the word 'Scripture' in the Bible means the Old Testament, because when Paul was writing his letter, the New Testament hadn't been put together. He wanted the Livewires to help show how the Bible as we know it today actually came about.

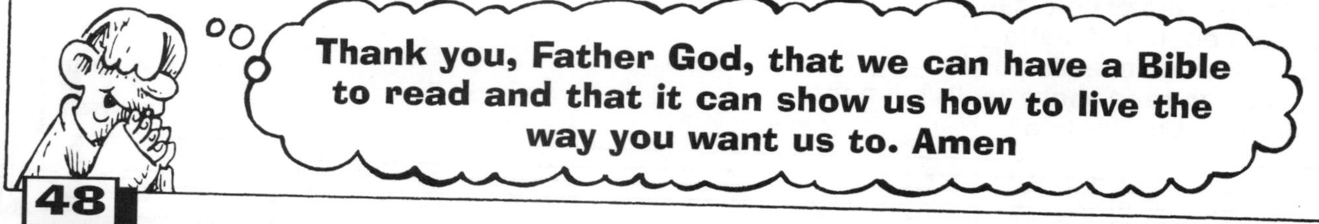
Thank you, Father God, that we can have a Bible to read and that it can show us how to live the way you want us to. Amen

Before the Livewires started on their own research and preparation, Dave told them about some of the people who had helped over the years to write, copy, translate and print the Bible so that people could have a copy. He told them that over many years people had worked hard, even risking their lives to write the Bible out in a language that could be understood by more people, as they thought it was important for people to be able to read it for themselves.

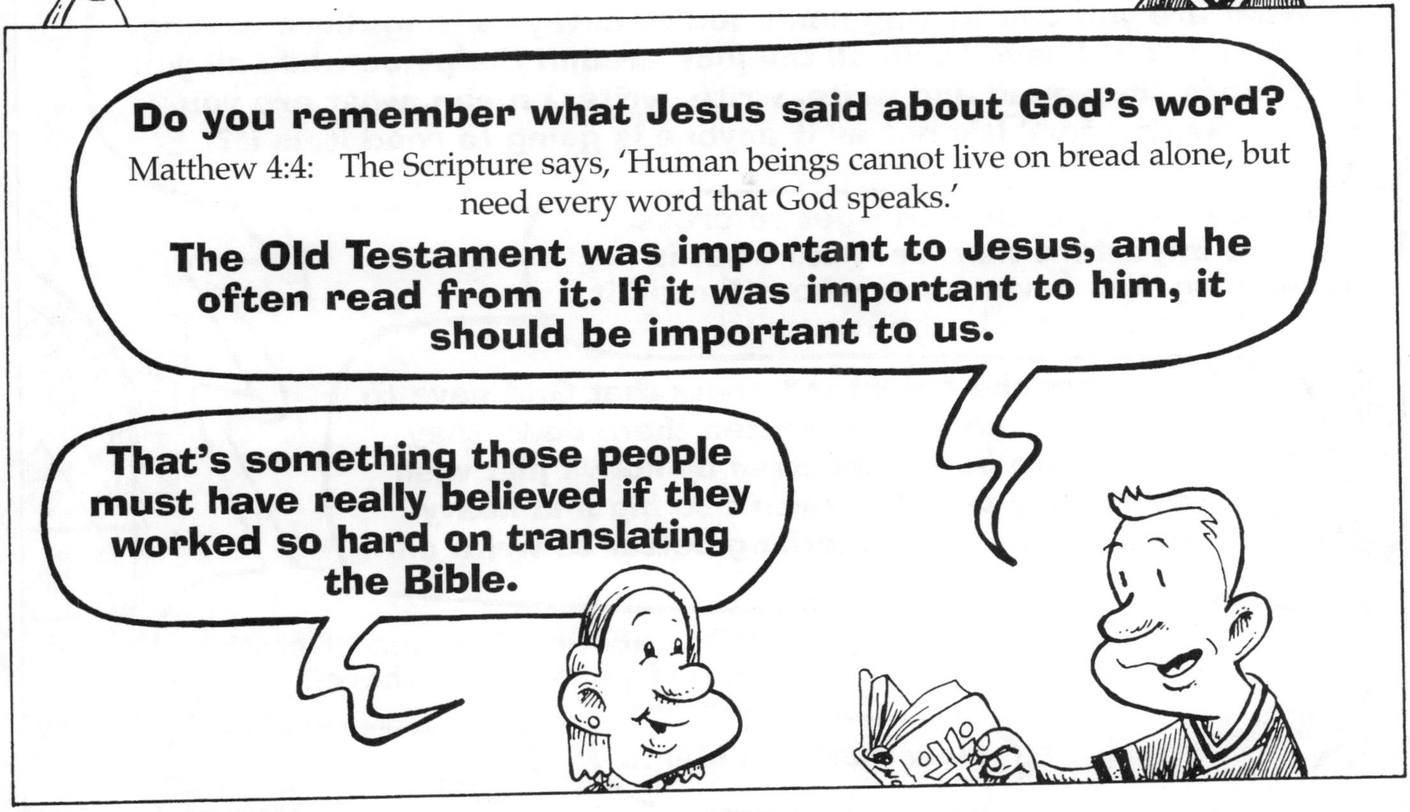

Do you remember what Jesus said about God's word?
Matthew 4:4: The Scripture says, 'Human beings cannot live on bread alone, but need every word that God speaks.'
The Old Testament was important to Jesus, and he often read from it. If it was important to him, it should be important to us.
That's something those people must have really believed if they worked so hard on translating the Bible.

As soon as Dave left them they enlisted Boot's help to give them the information they thought they might need. As they scrolled through, they found lots of facts about the way people first wrote things down, what they wrote on and how the Bible was eventually written in English. There were an awful lot of people involved!

They were going to be busy over the next few weeks.

The books of the Old Testament were originally written in Hebrew and later translated into Greek. The books of the New Testament were originally written in Greek. Can you guess what these words mean?

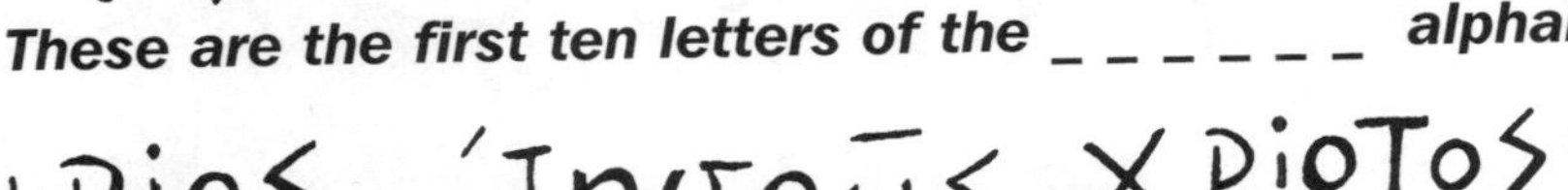

These are the first ten letters of the _ _ _ _ _ _ alphabet

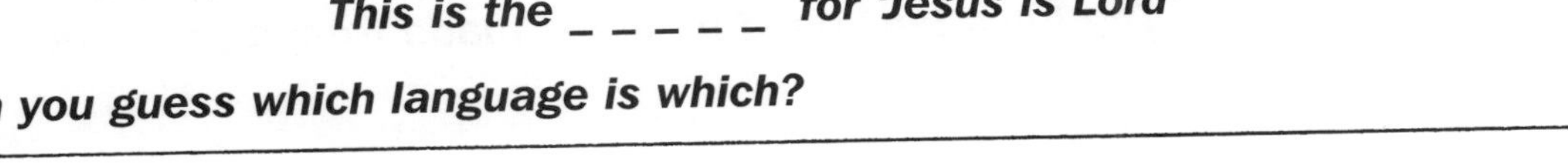

This is the _ _ _ _ _ for 'Jesus is Lord'

Can you guess which language is which?

The first day of the holiday club had arrived. The Livewires were feeling nervous about their first performance. They had worked very hard over the last few weeks and hoped that the children would enjoy and learn something from their presentation.

They admired each other's costumes. Digit, Tim and Quartz were doing the first sketch.

Soon they could hear Dave announcing them. They were on! All the children were sitting on the floor waiting.
Digit and Tim were writing on pieces of stone like clay tablets.
What are you two writing now? You're always sitting there writing. It's not fair. I have to do all the jobs around the place while all you do is sit around and write, write, write. I mean, what are you writing for? It's not as if anyone is going to read it, is it?
Now, now, my dear, don't get so cross. It is important that we write what is happening. You never know who will read it some time in the future.
Remember the commandments that God gave to Moses? If he hadn't written them down they would have been forgotten by now. I just wish these clay tablets weren't so big and heavy. Perhaps I'll invent something better to write on...
Oh yeah! What about this piece of cloth? You could get a lot on there!!
Now that's an idea...

Digit stepped forward and told the audience that before paper had been invented people used to write on pottery or tablets of clay. The Egyptians used papyrus, made from a plant, but this was expensive.

Now it was the turn of the other three Livewires to present their sketch.

Little Ben was dressed as a shepherd from Palestine about 50 years ago.

About 50 years ago, a shepherd was busy looking after his sheep when he discovered something pretty important.
Look what I've found! Look! What are they? I found them in a cave by the Dead Sea.
They opened them up and discovered scrolls. They looked very old and they wondered what they were. They sent them to some archaeologists. These are people who find out how people lived in the past.
Er, yes. These do look important. Now let me see. Oh yes! Yes! My goodness me, these can tell us a lot! I am so glad you found them.
But what are they?
You have found copies of the books of the Old Testament which are thousands of years old. They are older than any others we have.
The scrolls were made out of papyrus sheets and were rolled up for storage. This was a very important discovery. The writers of the Old Testament used scrolls. Listen to this verse...
Jeremiah 36:2: Get a scroll and write on it everything that I have told you about Israel and Judah and all the nations.

Everyone started clapping and the Livewires breathed a sigh of relief that their first presentation was over. Only four more to go!

Perhaps you could make a scroll and write a message on it.

Sticky tape
Paper
Cardboard tube
Roll!

On the second day of the holiday club the Livewires were ready for their next performance. Tim, Little Ben and Annie-log were on first. Tim and Little Ben were holding the scrolls they had made the day before. They heard all the children settle down and Dave was announcing them. They were on!

Tim and Little Ben sat on the floor writing on their scrolls. Annie-log, looking very important, strolled up to them.

I do hope you are not wasting time talking. I don't want any mistakes made this time.
We wouldn't dare make mistakes copying out the Scriptures. They are far too important.
Of course not! People check our work very carefully after we have checked it thoroughly ourselves.

Good! Just make sure that there are no changes—not even in the smallest letter, the 'jot'. We want people who read these words to know they are reading the truth.

Annie-log then read some words of Jesus...

Matthew 5:18:
Remember that as long as heaven and earth last, not the least point nor the smallest detail of the law will be done away with—not until the end of all things.

Annie-log then told the children that a scribe was a bit like our solicitors today. Some scribes worked for the government and others had the important job of copying out the Scriptures. They had to make sure they did not make any mistakes. Another scribe would often check the whole scroll.

You could now be a scribe and correct this verse on the scroll. The scribe who copied it down did not see the first letter of any of the words. Can you put them in?

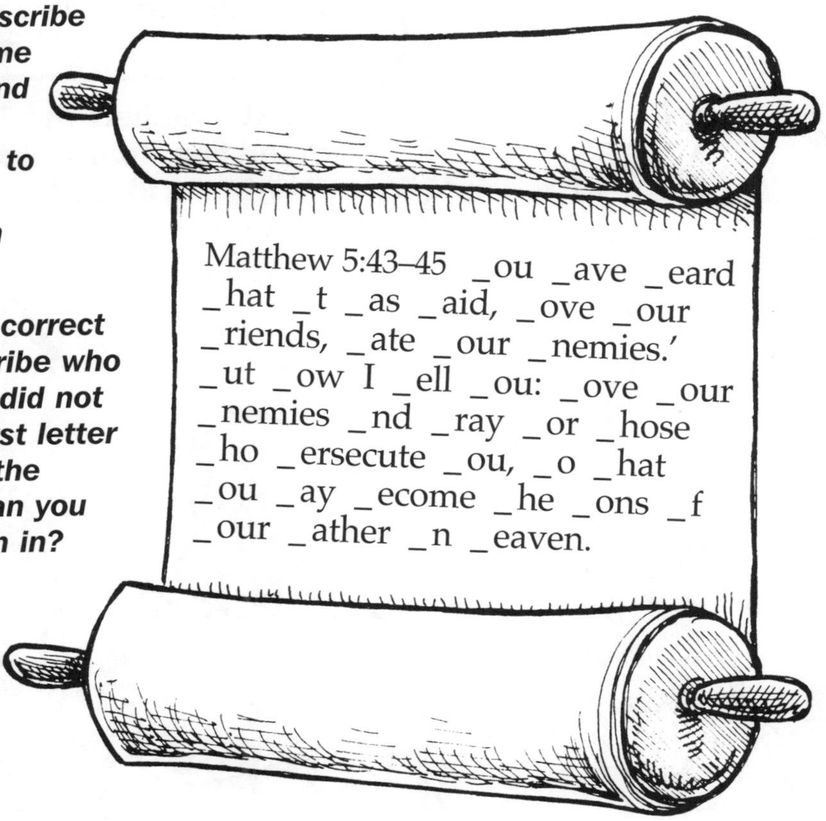
Matthew 5:43–45 _ou _ave _eard _hat _t _as _aid, _ove _our _riends, _ate _our _nemies.' _ut _ow I _ell _ou: _ove _our _nemies _nd _ray _or _hose _ho _ersecute _ou, _o _hat _ou _ay _ecome _he _ons _f _our _ather _n _eaven.

As Little Ben, Tim and Annie-log walked off stage, Data, Digit and Quartz walked on, dressed as monks. Digit had tried to make himself look fat! They sat on chairs and began writing using a quill pen. These pens were made out of swans' feathers. The end of the feather was sharpened to make a nib.

Good! I have nearly finished writing out Psalm 23—with no mistakes this time. Yesterday I had almost got to the end of Psalm 22 and the bell went for us to go to chapel. When I got back, I started writing out the same line again! I was so cross because I had to start all over again.
I hope I finish this bit before the ink runs out. I don't want to have to get the soot and egg white to make more.
I've just finished the illuminated letter for Psalm 46. Do you like it?
G

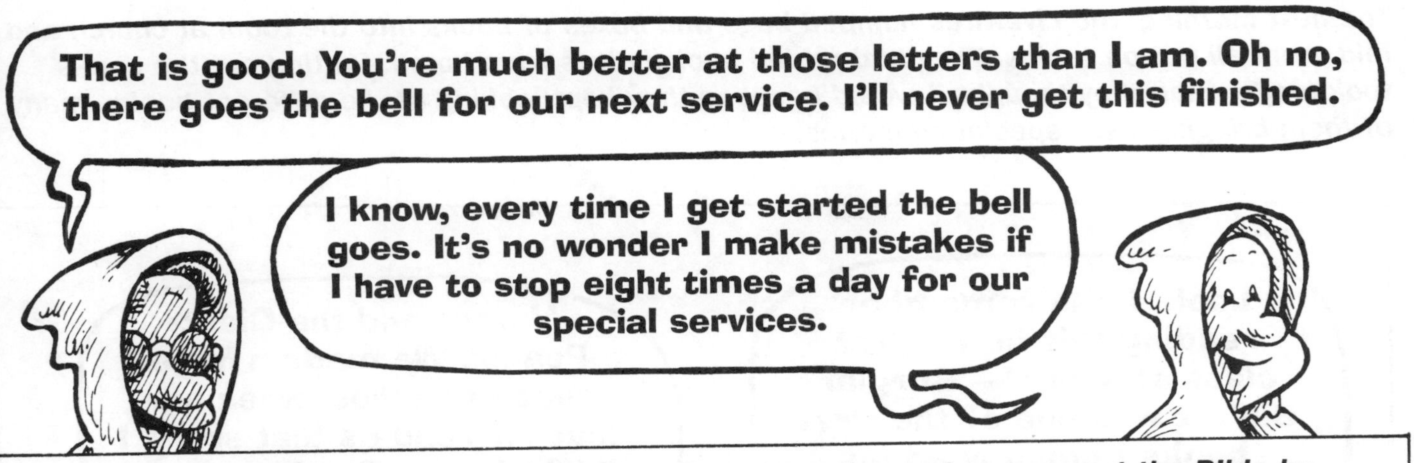
That is good. You're much better at those letters than I am. Oh no, there goes the bell for our next service. I'll never get this finished.
I know, every time I get started the bell goes. It's no wonder I make mistakes if I have to stop eight times a day for our special services.

Quartz told the children that hundreds of years ago, monks used to copy out the Bible by hand. This took a very long time to do. The monks tried to make them as beautiful as possible, and often decorated the pages and the first letters of chapters.

As the children go to make up their own illuminated letters you could design a special 'T' to go at the beginning of this verse—Psalm 23:1.

he Lord is my shepherd;
I have everything I need.

The next morning, the Livewires humped bags and boxes of books into the room at church and laid them all out on tables. They had raided bookshelves from home. Putting out the books took longer than they thought it would because they kept looking at the different books, many of them bringing back special memories.

Soon all the children eagerly arrived. The Livewires asked them to wander around the room looking at all the different books. Some of them sat on the floor looking at the picture books, others read some of the nursery rhymes, while some children were looking up facts about the War and space. There were so many different types of books that everyone could find something he or she liked.

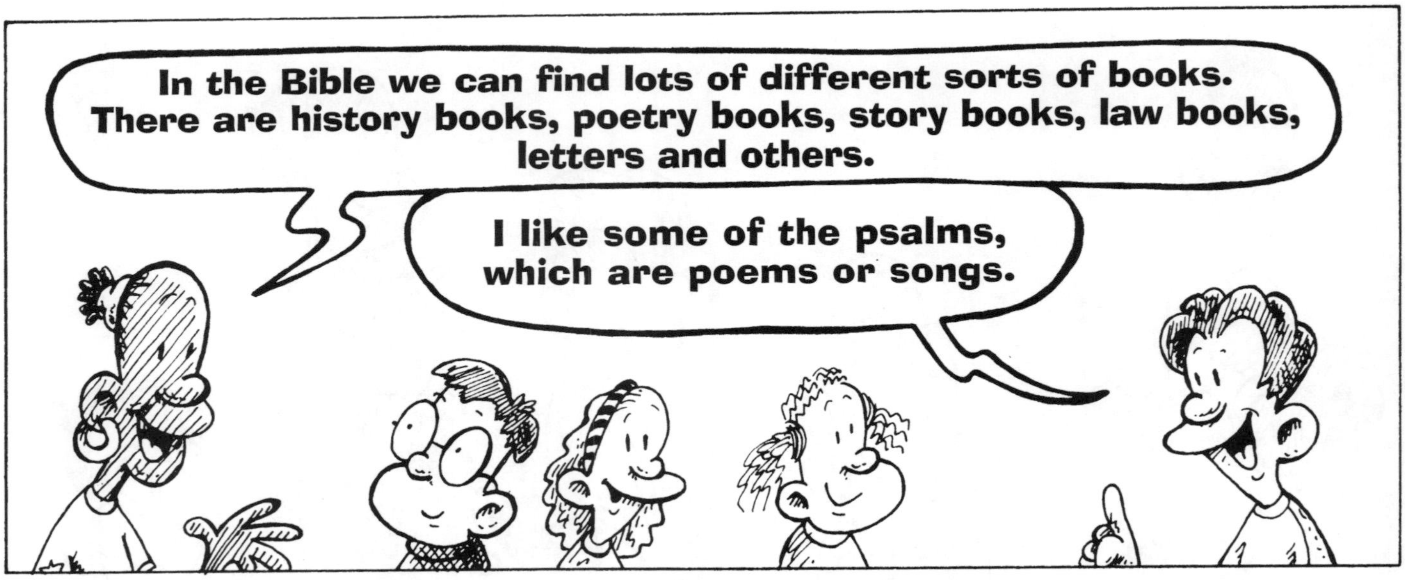

Look at your Bible library. Which books would you say are history or poetry books? Which are letters? Which books have the stories of Jesus told in them? You could give the different types of books different coloured spines.

Which book is your favourite?

The children started talking about the sorts of books they liked. One liked reading the Guinness Book of Records because he liked unusual facts, another enjoyed looking at pictures and making up her own story, while someone else preferred funny stories.

The Livewires told the children that the Bible contained lots of the stories Jesus told. Some of these were called parables. When Jesus told stories he often spoke in picture language to make it easier for the people to understand.

Tim and Digit then acted out one of the stories of Jesus. Perhaps you can guess which story it is.

It's hard work, this building, isn't it? I don't know how long it will take me to finish the foundations, but my dad always said to make sure the foundations were strong.
You don't want to worry too much about foundations—I don't. There's too much fuss about foundations.

Soon the other house was finished and they were both settling in happily, when there was an amazing storm which led to flooding. Soon there was a knock on one of the doors.
SCRIPT
Please can I come in? My house has fallen down—the foundations weren't strong enough!
Matthew 7:24: So then anyone who hears these words of mine and obeys them is like the wise man who built his house on the rock.

While the children go to make bookmarks you may like to make one too. You could write the words of today's verse on it and draw a picture of the two builders.

The Livewires could hardly believe that the holiday club was almost over. Quartz and Little Ben, with Bibles hung around their necks, walked on to the stage.

I say we burn them, with their Bibles. We don't want them reading these Bibles. They shouldn't be allowed. Burn them! Burn them! If only that man had not translated the Bible into English, none of this would have happened. He has a lot to answer for.
But what have we done wrong? We were only reading the Bible in English. What's wrong with that? We want to read it for ourselves.
At that point Annie-log came on to the stage.
Friends, I translated the Bible from Latin to English because I thought it was important for ordinary people to read the Bible for themselves, and not just rely on what the clergy in the church were saying. It took me a long time, but my curate, John Purvey, helped. Even though I was ill, I did not want to give up.

Little Ben then explained that the one Bible that John Wycliffe had copied had to be copied and re-copied. They were sent all over the country. Men took them into villages and, because not many people could read, they read to them. Little Ben read a verse he thought might have helped John Wycliffe.

James 1:12: Happy is the person who remains faithful under trials, because when he succeeds in passing such a test, he will receive as his reward the life which God has promised to those who love him.

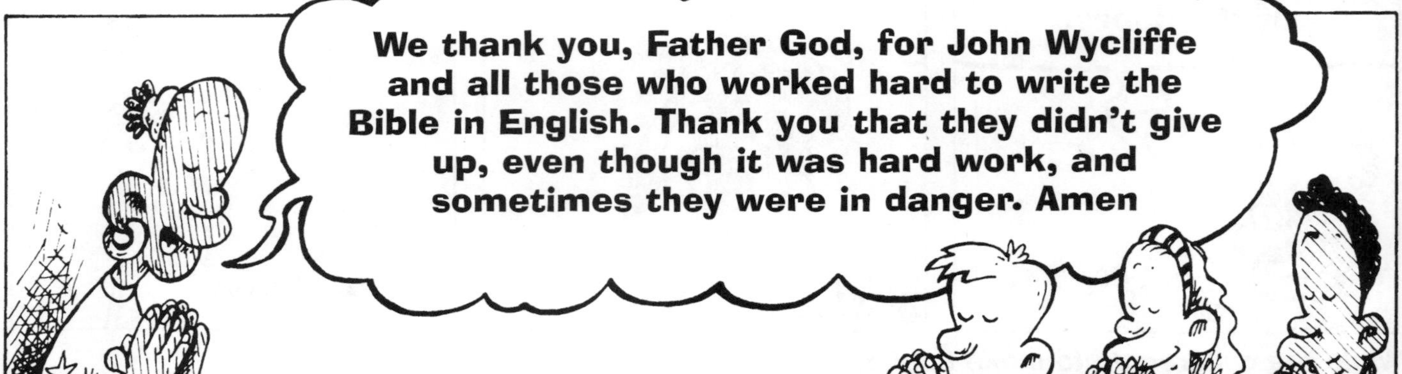
We thank you, Father God, for John Wycliffe and all those who worked hard to write the Bible in English. Thank you that they didn't give up, even though it was hard work, and sometimes they were in danger. Amen

Quartz said this prayer while everyone was sitting quietly.

After waiting for a few moments Tim stepped forward carrying a large poster.
Look over there!
Wonder what's happened? Let's go and see.
Why is he wanted?
What has he done?
I'll tell you what he's done. He has been translating the Greek New Testament into English! That's not allowed.
WANTED! WILLIAM TYNDALE

After John Wycliffe died the preachers were stopped from selling the Bible, and once again the people did not have a Bible to read in English because no one was allowed to translate.
That is, until someone else brave enough to risk his life came along. William Tyndale, who was a clever man, spent many years translating the New Testament from Greek into English. He went to Germany to finish his work because he was afraid he would be found out.
Tyndale did finish his work and he managed to get it printed before he was finally betrayed by a spy. He was put in prison before being burnt at the stake. His last words were 'Open the King of England's eyes.'

The children went off to design their own 'Wanted' posters for William Tyndale. You could make your own. Write this verse from Psalm 31 on the poster, which describes William Tyndale:

Psalm 31:24: Be strong, be courageous, all you that hope in the Lord.

The final day had arrived! Thankfully it was a sunny day because the Livewires had arranged an outdoor event. They were going to have a treasure hunt which everyone was looking forward to.

When they arrived at the park the Livewires told them the rules. Around the park were two types of clue, pictures of different things and Bible verses, which had to be matched up.

Eagerly they set off. The Livewires sat back and enjoyed watching the children run around finding the clues they had cleverly hidden.

I wonder if they'll find the one on the rose bush.
Or the one near the tennis courts.
I hope the pigeons don't eat the clue I put under the trees!

Soon they were back with all the clues. Can you help match them up?

There are two clues to why we should read the Bible in the picture above, to do with eating and seeing. Can you think what they might be?

As they were enjoying their food, one of the children looked very thoughtful, then suddenly shouted out...

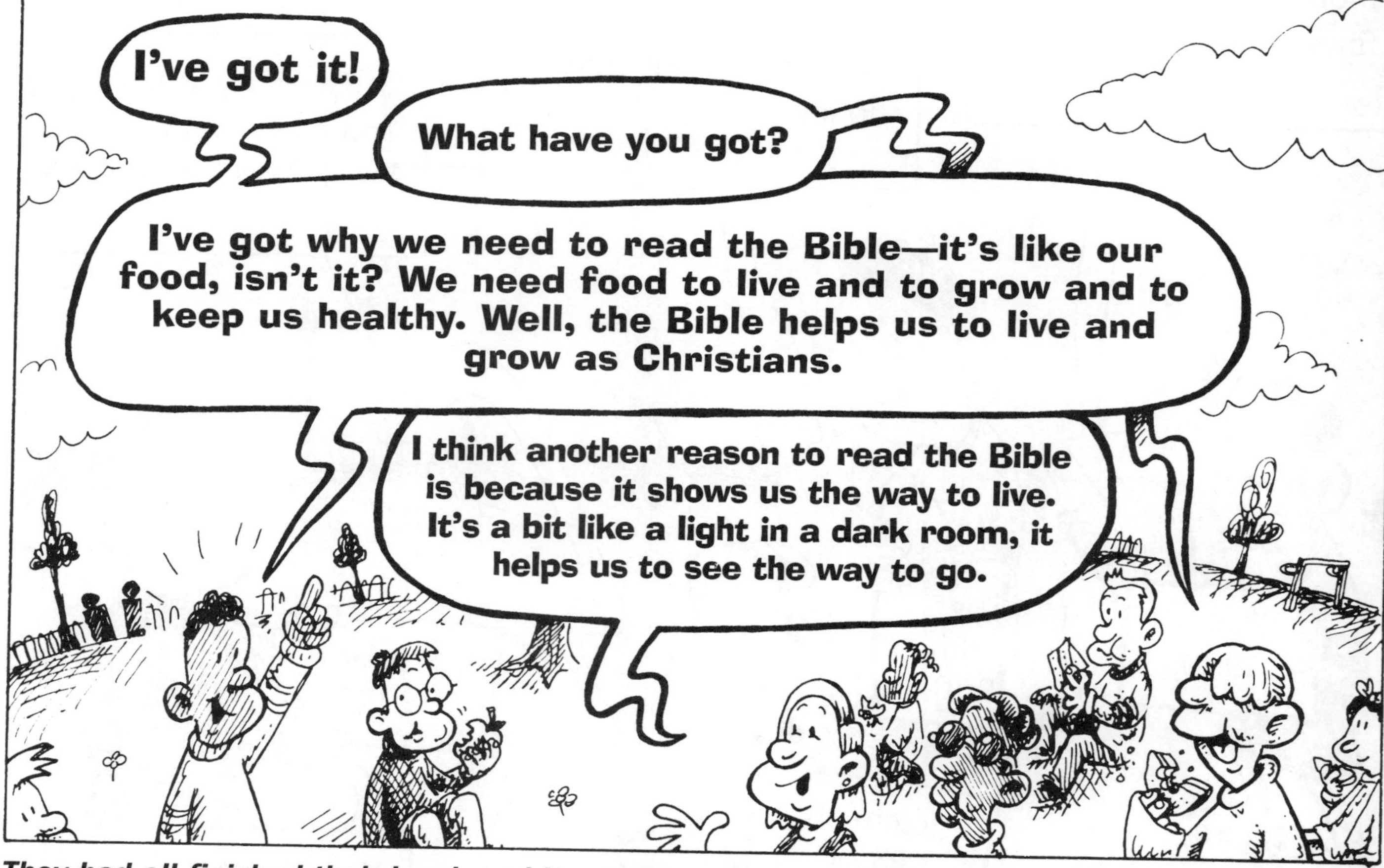

They had all finished their lunch and it was time to get on with the last part of the treasure hunt. Although they had found the clues, they had not found the treasure. The Livewires gave them a few more clues. Can you work out where and what the treasure is from them?

There was much discussion about where and what it could be. They asked the Livewires if it was in the park and when they said 'no' they all went back to the church.

At the church, Peter tore off to a cupboard behind the organ. In it he found a lunch box, which he brought out. On opening it he found the treasure inside—a Bible—with this verse written on it:

Psalm 119:18: Open my eyes that I may see the wonderful truths in your law.
BIBLE

Everyone sat in a circle and learnt the verse by saying a word each around the circle, getting faster and faster until they all knew it by heart.

See how fast you can say the verse. Can you learn it by heart?

F A C T F I L E

Before the children went home at the end of the day, there were lots of different activities for them to do. Here are some of them for you to try.

Design a cover for your own Bible.

Make up a wordsearch and include these words in it: TYNDALE, WYCLIFFE, FOOD, HONEY, LIGHT, TRANSLATE, CLAY, MONK, SCROLL, SCRIBE.

Make up a code for this Bible verse —it's one of my favourites.

Psalm 46:1: God is our shelter and strength, always ready to help in times of trouble.

Try this True or False quiz on your friends.

The Old Testament books were originally written in Greek.

Moses wrote the Ten Commandments on a scroll.

The Old Testament was important to Jesus.

We have not always had the Bible in English.

The Bible shows us how to live as Christians.

Or this word puzzle.

1. **Jesus would have read this** — O__ T________
2. **They copied the Scriptures on to scrolls** — S___
3. **Tyndale translated from this language** — G____
4. **Wycliffe translated from this language** — L____
5. **Tyndale fled to this country** — G______
6. **Monks wrote with this** — Q____

How many words can you make from the word Testament?